ASHES TO INSPIRATION

DR. SARATH KUMAR S

To my beloved wife, Jayu, whose unwavering love and support have been my guiding light through the darkest times. Your strength and grace inspire me daily, and I am forever grateful for your presence.

To my son, Satvik Sarath, whose innocence and joy bring light to every day. May you always find strength and happiness, no matter the challenges life presents.

To my dear friend Akhil, whose belief in the power of sharing my journey ignited the idea for this book. Thank you for inspiring me to offer hope to others.

To every individual facing adversity—may this book serve as a reminder that, no matter how difficult the road, we rise stronger together.

Contents

Contents

Contents

Foreword

In a world where challenges often seem insurmountable, this book emerges as a beacon of hope and resilience. It is not merely a collection of experiences; it is a testament to the human spirit's capacity to rise above adversity and embrace life with renewed vigor.

As a cancer survivor, the author takes us on a deeply personal journey, sharing the emotional upheaval of diagnosis, the weight of uncertainty, and the strength found in vulnerability. With each chapter, readers are invited to reflect on their own battles, no matter how big or small, and to recognize that the journey of healing is often a winding path filled with both struggle and triumph.

This book is for anyone who has ever felt lost, overwhelmed, or trapped by circumstances beyond their control. It serves as a reminder that even in our darkest moments, we have the power to redefine our narrative and cultivate resilience. The author's journey, filled with raw honesty and powerful insights, offers valuable lessons for navigating life's challenges and rediscovering hope.

May this book inspire you to embrace your own journey, to seek the light in the shadows, and to understand that every setback can be a setup for a comeback. The road may be long, but with courage and determination, we can all rise from the ashes.

Preface

Life often unfolds in ways we never anticipate, confronting us with challenges that demand strength and resilience we might not know we possess. When I was diagnosed with cancer, my world came to a sudden halt. In that moment, I was thrust into a journey of pain, fear, and ultimately, profound self-discovery. This book is born from that journey—a journey of battling not only illness but also the inner struggles that accompany life's most difficult trials.

Ashes to Inspiration is more than a recounting of my own experiences. It's an invitation for each of you to find your own path to healing and empowerment. Whether you face challenges with health, relationships, career, or finances, I hope these pages offer you a sense of comfort and encouragement. This book combines my personal story with reflections, insights, and practical steps that I have found helpful along the way. Through sharing this, my intention is to remind you that, regardless of the depths to which we may fall, there is always a way to rise.

Writing this book has been a transformative experience. In putting my journey into words, I've realized that resilience isn't a destination; it's a process of continual growth. I invite you to walk this path with me, to see that every setback has the potential to fuel a comeback, and to recognize the power that lies within each of us to create meaningful change.

Thank you for joining me in this journey of strength, healing, and renewal.

With hope and resilience,
Sarath Kumar S

Acknowledgements

This book would not have been possible without the unwavering support and love of my family, friends, and colleagues.

To my beloved wife, Jayu—your strength and resilience have been my greatest sources of inspiration. You've stood by me through every trial and triumph, and your love has been a light guiding me forward. I am forever grateful to you.

To my son, Satvik Sarath, who fills my life with joy and reminds me of life's simple beauties. Your innocence and laughter gave me purpose and a renewed will to fight through each day.

To our families, including Jayu's, whose encouragement and love carried me through the darkest times. You gave me the courage to continue, even when the journey felt overwhelming.

To my friends and colleagues, thank you for your words of encouragement, understanding, and kindness. Each message, each call, and each moment of compassion reminded me that I was never alone in this journey.

To those who chose not to speak, who turned away when they learned of my illness, thank you for showing me your true colors in adversity. Your silence has been as loud as the support of others, and it served as a powerful reminder of the strength that can be found in those who remain by your side.

And finally, to all the readers who may face their own battles—may this book serve as a reminder that hope exists, even in the hardest of times, and that no journey is taken in vain.

With gratitude and appreciation,
Sarath Kumar S

Prologue

The news came like a storm on a calm day. One moment, I was navigating the rhythms of everyday life, working in a foreign country, making plans, and dreaming of the future. The next, I was sitting in a sterile room, listening to words that would change everything. "You have cancer," the doctor said, his voice steady and clinical. In that instant, my world shifted, every expectation and goal I'd held flickered and wavered like a candle in the wind.

As I faced this unexpected journey, I wrestled with emotions I hadn't felt before—fear, anger, despair. I grappled with the desire to shield my loved ones, to protect them from the pain and uncertainty I felt. Yet, through each struggle, a quiet resilience began to rise within me. I realized that this battle was as much a journey of the spirit as it was a physical fight for survival.

Ashes to Inspiration is not just my story; it is a story of human strength, of rising even when everything seems to be crumbling. Through this book, I share the moments of doubt, the flashes of hope, and the small victories that paved my way forward. Each chapter is a reflection on resilience, an invitation to embrace the challenges life brings, and a reminder that even in our darkest hours, we can find light.

This prologue marks the beginning of a journey—a journey of transformation, healing, and renewal. My hope is that, through sharing my experiences, I can offer strength to others walking through their own storms, facing their own battles. We all carry within us the ability to rise from the ashes.

CHAPTER I

A Sudden Shift

The antiseptic smell of the hospital hung heavily in the air, a constant reminder of the vulnerability that had entered my life. I sat alone in the waiting room, my heart racing as I clutched the edge of the chair, staring at the stark white walls. Time felt suspended, each tick of the clock amplifying the silence around me.

Just seven months ago, I had arrived in Qatar, full of hope and ambition, ready to embrace a new chapter in my career. I had immersed myself in the fast-paced lifestyle, excited about the opportunities ahead. Now, however, I found myself grappling with a reality I never imagined I would face.

After what felt like an eternity, the door creaked open, and the doctor stepped in. His serious yet compassionate expression sent a chill through me.

"Mr. Sarath, the results have come in," he said, his tone steady. "You have cancer." The words crashed over me like a wave, leaving me momentarily breathless. The world around me faded as I struggled to process the enormity of what I had just heard.

"It's best that you return to India and continue your treatment there," he advised gently. As the gravity of his words sank in, a flood of emotions washed over me—fear, disbelief, and a profound sense of loss for the life I had been building just a short time before.

I reflected on my journey over the past seven months: the late nights at work, the new friendships formed, and the dreams I had nurtured. All of it felt so distant now, overshadowed by this sudden diagnosis. The thought of leaving Qatar, a place that had once promised so much, filled me with a deep ache. Yet, in that moment of despair, I also felt a flicker of determination igniting within me.

As the doctor detailed the next steps, I resolved to confront this challenge head-on. I was ready to fight—not just for my health but for the future I still believed was possible. I took a deep breath, steeling myself for the journey ahead. This was my path, and I would rise from this moment, no matter how daunting it seemed.

CHAPTER II

A Heart Divided

As I turned away from the doctor's office, the reality of my diagnosis weighed heavily on my shoulders. The sterile hallway stretched out before me, but my mind was miles away, consumed with thoughts of my wife, Jayu, and our four-year-old son, Satvik. Their faces flooded my memory, bright and full of life, and a deep ache settled in my chest.

How could I explain this to them? How would they handle the news that I was facing such a daunting battle? I could already envision the concern in Jayu's eyes, the way her smile might falter as she absorbed the weight of my words. My heart tightened at the thought of how this would affect our family, the future we had envisioned together suddenly shrouded in uncertainty.

Walking toward my hospital room felt surreal. Each step echoed with my fears and hopes, the emotions swirling within me like a storm. Would I still be the father Satvik needed? The husband Jayu deserved? My mind raced through countless scenarios, each more daunting than the last. I pictured Satvik's innocent laughter, the way he would run into my arms after a long day at work, and the moments we shared as a family. I couldn't bear the thought of leaving them behind, of being unable to provide for them or be present in their lives.

Once I reached my room, I took a moment to collect myself. The walls felt close, the fluorescent lights buzzing overhead. I sank into the chair by the window and looked out at the world beyond. The view was a stark contrast to my inner turmoil—people bustling about, living their lives while I felt trapped in this moment of uncertainty.

I pulled out my phone, staring at pictures of my family. There was one of Jayu and Satvik at the beach, their faces lit up with joy, their laughter echoing in my mind. I couldn't let this diagnosis define our future. I had to fight—not just for myself, but for them.

As I sat in that quiet room, I made a silent promise to myself: I would embrace this challenge with every ounce of strength I possessed. I would face this cancer with the same determination that I had brought to my career and life in Qatar. I was not just fighting for my health; I was fighting for my family's future, their happiness, and the dreams we had yet to fulfill together.

CHAPTER III

A Silent Departure

Stepping out of the doctor's cabin felt like crossing into an unexpected reality. The weight of my diagnosis pressed on me, but I chose not to reveal the truth to my family. Instead, I fabricated a story about stomach issues, saying I needed to return to Kerala for better treatment. I couldn't bear to see Jayu's anxious eyes or Satvik's innocent questions, so I cloaked myself in silence, determined to shield them from the harsh reality.

As COVID-19 began to spread, the urgency to leave grew stronger. Flights were becoming scarce, and each moment felt uncertain. I reached out to my management, revealing my cancer diagnosis and explaining the situation. Their reaction—a mix of shock and encouragement—was unexpectedly comforting. They wished me well and assured me my position would be waiting when I returned healthy, which fueled my resolve to fight.

I informed my friend and roommate, Akhil, and my colleague, Ancy, about my plans. Their support during this turbulent time was invaluable. Ancy, using her contacts, worked tirelessly to arrange a flight for me. The thought of going home stirred mixed emotions; I longed to see my family, yet I felt burdened by the secret I carried.

Finally, the day of departure came. Akhil accompanied me to the airport, and before I went inside, he hugged me tightly—a silent gesture filled with unspoken words and mixed emotions that I knew I would carry with me for a lifetime. It was a moment of friendship and support in the face of uncertainty, one that would forever remind me of the connections holding me up.

As I entered the airport, emotions surged within me. The streets of Qatar, once full of life and opportunity, felt different now—a bittersweet memory of a life I was about to leave behind. I could see the apprehension in the eyes of other travelers. Masks had become the new norm, and social distancing measures were in place. It felt surreal amidst so much global uncertainty, yet I pressed forward, focused on the journey ahead.

CHAPTER IV

A Race Against Time

As I sat in the terminal, my anxiety began to swell. The airport was eerily quiet, with the usual buzz of travelers replaced by an unsettling silence. With the COVID-19 pandemic in full swing, boarding announcements were few and far between, and I felt a growing sense of unease. Time slipped away unnoticed, and before I realized it, my flight to Kochi was called, but I was still waiting for the announcement that never came.

When the reality struck that I had missed my flight, panic surged through me. I rushed to the boarding gate, only to find it closed and the flight already departed. The weight of my situation pressed heavily on my chest; I was already feeling vulnerable, and this felt like a cruel twist of fate.

Desperate, I approached the airport staff, explaining my predicament. They listened, their expressions a mix of concern and understanding. I pulled out the medical documents from the doctor, the proof of my condition, and watched as the staff deliberated among themselves. The urgency in my voice was palpable, and I could see them weighing their options.

After what felt like an eternity, one of the staff members returned to me with a determined look. "We can arrange another flight for you," she said, and relief washed over me. I was grateful for their willingness to help. In a time when so many were filled with fear, the compassion shown by these individuals was a beacon of hope.

With their assistance, I was quickly rebooked on a later flight. As I settled into my seat and prepared for takeoff, I reflected on the challenges of the day. The stress of traveling during a pandemic, coupled with the weight of my diagnosis, had pushed me to my limits. Yet, somehow, I had persevered.

As the plane ascended into the sky, I closed my eyes and took a deep breath. I thought about my family waiting for me in Kerala. I reminded myself that every hurdle I faced was part of this journey, one that I was determined to navigate. I was not just a passenger on a flight; I was a warrior ready to face whatever lay ahead.

CHAPTER V

Homeward Bound

As the plane touched down at Kochi Airport, a wave of mixed emotions washed over me. It was around 7 PM, and the night sky was blanketed with stars, a stark contrast to the turmoil I felt inside. I was relieved to have finally arrived in Kerala, yet the reality of my situation lingered like a shadow.

Upon disembarking, I was informed that my luggage would not arrive for another week, as it had been checked in on a different flight. It was a small setback, but at that moment, I was just grateful to be back home, where my family awaited me. With COVID-19 protocols in place, the airport felt surreal—empty, quiet, and filled with masked faces. I navigated through the terminal with a heightened sense of caution, aware that this journey was unlike any I had experienced before.

Stepping outside the airport, I felt the warm, familiar breeze of Kerala envelop me, bringing a sense of comfort amidst the uncertainty. I quickly secured a taxi, taking extra precautions to ensure my safety during the ride. The driver, though wearing a mask, greeted me with a nod, and we set off toward Kottayam, my heart racing with anticipation and anxiety.

The road stretched before us, flanked by lush greenery and the faint sounds of the night. Yet, my mind was a torrent of thoughts. I couldn't wait to see Jayu and Satvik, but I was also acutely aware of the secret I was carrying. I imagined their faces lighting up upon seeing me, but fear crept in—how would I explain my absence, the urgency of my return, without revealing the true nature of my condition?

With each passing kilometer, memories of my family flooded my mind—Satvik's laughter, Jayu's unwavering support. They were my motivation, the reason I had made this difficult journey home. I promised myself that I would face this battle not just for me, but for them.

As we neared Kottayam, I felt a mix of relief and trepidation. I was ready to embrace my family, yet the weight of my diagnosis loomed over me. I took a deep breath, gathering my strength for what lay ahead. This was just the beginning of my fight, and no matter how challenging the road ahead, I was determined to rise from this experience, stronger than ever.

CHAPTER VI

Close Yet Apart

Reaching Kerala felt like clearing the first hurdle in a long, grueling race. But the homecoming I'd envisioned was immediately cut short by COVID-19 restrictions. I rented a house close to Jayu's home for my isolation period, where she and my mother-in-law waited for my arrival. As I stepped in, I caught a glimpse of them standing outside, mixed emotions stirring within me. Knowing I wouldn't see Jayu's face for a long time, I urged her to return home and reassured her that I'd already eaten dinner at the airport.

For the next 30 days, isolation became my reality, cutting me off from the warmth and presence of my family. Each hour felt endless as I wrestled with both my illness and the emotions that surfaced daily. The pain was more than physical; it was a loneliness that seeped into every corner of my mind. Yet, I held on to the hope of reuniting with my family.

Jayu's daily visits soon became my lifeline. Every morning, she would bring breakfast, and later lunch and dinner, standing outside the house just to see me, her smile filled with reassurance. I knew she bore her own heartache, staying strong for me, and in those quiet moments of shared silence, I felt an unspoken bond—a strength that kept me going, despite the physical and emotional strain.

My son, Satvik, remained blissfully unaware of the reality. He still believed I was in Qatar, though he grew suspicious with each missed video call. I avoided those calls to protect him from seeing my pain, though the ache of separation weighed heavily on me. I held on to memories of his laughter, using them to fill the silence, reminding myself that one day, I would hold him again.

CHAPTER VII

The Revelation

It was on one of those long, isolated nights in the rented house that I decided it was finally time to tell Jayu the truth. The secret had weighed heavily on me, and each passing day of separation made it harder to keep it from her. Taking a deep breath, I picked up the phone and called her. When she answered, her voice was soft, hopeful—a sound that brought me comfort.

I took a moment, then gently began, "Jayu, there's something I need to tell you..." I could hear her breath hitch as I told her about my diagnosis, revealing the truth I'd hidden in order to protect her and Satvik.

She fell silent, the shock hitting her, and then I heard her cry. It was a sound that broke my heart—a mix of fear, sorrow, and helplessness. My own emotions surged, but I stayed calm, speaking softly. "Please don't worry," I said, trying to reassure her, though the words felt inadequate against her pain. "I'm fighting this, and I'll come out of it. We'll get through this together."

In that moment, her vulnerability mirrored my own, yet her strength emerged through her tears. She spoke with a trembling voice, expressing her fears, yet underneath was the love and resilience I'd come to cherish. I felt a deep, unspoken bond between us, a determination that, even in the face of the unknown, we would support each other through this journey.

Her daily visits continued, now filled with even more love and concern. Each meal she brought, every smile she managed through her tears, became a reminder of why I was fighting. Our bond was stronger than ever, and even in this challenging time, I drew strength from her support.

CHAPTER VIII

Voices Through the Void

In the quiet isolation of my rented house, my connection to the world outside came through the voices of two people who became my lifeline: Akhil and Ancy. Every day, their calls and messages brought a spark of comfort, breaking the silence that had wrapped itself around me.

Akhil's daily phone calls were a balm, each conversation filled with humor, shared memories, and encouragement. He never spoke directly about my illness, sensing that what I needed most was not a reminder of my condition, but a reminder of the life that awaited me once I was well. He would talk about our favorite places, or a movie he'd watched, and in those moments, I felt grounded. It was like he was pulling me out of isolation, one laugh, one story at a time. Through his words, I found the strength to believe that a day would come when I'd be able to leave this house and return to the world.

Ancy, who I thought of as an elder sister, was a constant source of comfort. Her WhatsApp messages were always filled with warmth and encouragement, as if she were right there beside me. She checked on me morning and night, her words a reminder that someone cared deeply about my journey. She often shared prayers, hopeful words, and small pieces of advice, urging me to stay strong. Her presence brought a calmness that soothed even the worst of my fears.

Some nights, Akhil would call just to make sure I wasn't feeling alone, and other times, he and Ancy would both send funny pictures or inspiring quotes. It was as though they had formed an invisible circle around me, their support a shield I hadn't even known I needed.

In those shared moments of connection, I found a way to endure. They reminded me that, even in isolation, friendship and family could reach across any distance, weaving a web of strength and support that held me up when I felt close to breaking. Through their calls and messages, Akhil and Ancy became more than friends—they became my lifeline, keeping my spirit alive, day by day.

CHAPTER IX

Breaking the Barrier

The days were blurring into one another, a cycle of quiet endurance and waiting. Jayu continued her daily visits, bringing food and the strength of her presence. I had come to accept the distance between us and my isolation, telling myself it was only temporary, a necessary measure for the safety of everyone I loved.

But then, one afternoon, I heard a sound that shattered the quiet—a small voice, calling out, "Appa." For a second, I froze, thinking it must be a trick of the mind. But there it was again, stronger this time, "Appa!" I looked down from the window and saw my son, Satvik, standing next to Jayu. His wide, curious eyes looked up, as if waiting for me to appear.

In that moment, all the barriers and rules around us melted away. Before I knew it, I was at the door, and Satvik had run up to me, wrapping his small arms around me. I forgot every restriction, every protocol, and simply held him, feeling his heartbeat against mine. I hadn't realized how much I had missed that feeling until now. He looked up at me with a determination that seemed far beyond his years, and said, "I will not leave you now, Appa. I'll be with you always."

His words filled me with a strength I hadn't felt in months. The comfort of holding him, the love he radiated, renewed my will to fight. After that day, everything changed. I no longer had to carry the weight alone; my family was my strength, and they were by my side, regardless of the circumstances. The remaining days of quarantine felt lighter, knowing that each day brought me closer to recovery, and I could finally face the next steps with the ones I loved beside me.

18

CHAPTER X

The Hospital Visit

After 30 long days of isolation, I finally felt a glimmer of hope at the prospect of starting my treatment. The fatigue weighed on me, and I knew I needed professional help. With Jayu and my father-in-law by my side, we made our way to Caritas Hospital, feeling both anxious and hopeful. The thought of beginning my journey toward recovery filled me with anticipation.

However, upon arrival, reality hit hard. Due to the stringent COVID-19 protocols in place, the hospital staff informed us that I would not be allowed to enter the hospital. The regulations were strict for those returning from abroad, and they couldn't make exceptions, no matter how desperate my situation felt.

I explained my circumstances to the staff, detailing the pain I was enduring and the urgency of my need for treatment. They listened patiently, but the rules were clear. Instead, they directed Jayu and me to a small, isolated room in a corner of the hospital. We sat there, waiting for what felt like an eternity—four hours filled with uncertainty and anxiety.

When Dr. Unni finally arrived, the weight of those hours was almost unbearable. I remember his calm demeanor and the empathy in his eyes, which immediately put me at ease. He assessed my situation thoroughly, understanding the depth of my suffering. Although the news was disheartening—he explained that due to my recent travels and the need to adhere to the protocols, he could not proceed with the necessary tests—his presence was a source of reassurance.

"Come back after 30 days," he advised gently, "and then we can proceed with the tests." His words, though not what I wanted to hear, were delivered with such care and compassion that they didn't feel like a dismissal but a promise that help was on the horizon. I remember feeling a sense of relief just knowing that Dr. Unni was there, committed to my care. His kindness and patience were a bright light in that moment of uncertainty.

As we left the hospital, my heart sank. The thought of enduring more weeks of pain without a clear path to treatment was overwhelming. Yet, I leaned on the strength of my wife, who held my hand tightly as we walked back to the auto. In that moment, I realized that even amidst the struggles, I wasn't alone. Jayu's unwavering support became my anchor, reminding me that I had to keep fighting, no matter how long the road ahead appeared.

And I knew that when the time was right, Dr. Unni would be there to help me take the next step in my recovery. His dedication to my well-being had already given me hope—something I desperately needed in those moments of doubt.

CHAPTER XI

The Long Awaited Tests

After enduring 60 grueling days of isolation, I returned to the hospital, my body a mere shadow of its former self. Painkillers had been my constant companions, dulling the edge of the agony but never truly alleviating it. Many nights, I would wake up to find myself unconscious on the floor, the world around me fading in and out, leaving me dizzy and disoriented. The continuous vomiting and unrelenting stomach pain had taken their toll; I felt as if every fiber of my being was collapsing under the weight of my illness.

As I walked into the unni doctor's office that day, I could feel my heart racing—not just from fear, but from a flicker of hope that maybe this visit would bring answers. The waiting room, once a place of dread, felt like a threshold to a new chapter, a chance to finally understand what I was facing.

The doctor, observing my condition, quickly noted the severity of my symptoms. "We need to conduct a PET scan and a biopsy to determine the severity and stage of the cancer," he said, his voice steady but filled with urgency. Those words sent a wave of emotions crashing over me—relief that I was finally getting the attention I needed, mixed with fear of what those results might reveal.

After what felt like an eternity of waiting, I underwent the PET scan. The procedure felt surreal, lying there as the machine whirred around me, capturing images of my body while I couldn't help but wonder about the shadows lurking within. The biopsy followed shortly after, a necessary step that felt like an intrusion into my already fragile state.

The next few days were a blur of anxiety. I returned home, my body wracked with pain, and the weight of uncertainty pressing down on me. My mind raced with thoughts of what the results might reveal. Each passing hour felt like a day as I awaited the call from the doctor. I clung to Jayu's hand during sleepless nights, her presence a balm for my racing thoughts. Together, we tried to stay hopeful, even as doubts crept in.

As the days turned into what felt like an eternity, I prepared myself for whatever news was coming. I had fought through so much already, and now it was time to face the truth—whatever it might be.

CHAPTER XII

The Shattering Diagnosis

The day I received the results felt like a storm had hit, turning my world upside down. As I sat in the sterile room, the doctor entered with a serious expression that immediately set my heart racing. I braced myself, preparing for the worst, but nothing could have truly prepared me for what came next.

"Mr. Sarath, you have been diagnosed with lymphoma, a type of blood cancer, and it is at stage four, which is advanced," he said, his voice steady but laced with compassion. Those words hung in the air, each syllable a heavy weight pressing down on my chest. A deep chill ran through me, and my mind raced as I processed the reality of the situation.

I glanced at Jayu, who was sitting next to me. Her eyes filled with tears as the news sank in, and she began to cry softly, the weight of it all crashing down on her. I felt a deep sorrow for her, for the pain this would bring to our family. But amidst the shock and despair, a fire ignited within me. I couldn't let this diagnosis define me; I had to find the strength to fight, not just for myself but for her and for Satvik.

I took a deep breath, gathering my thoughts. "We will get through this," I said, my voice more resolute than I felt inside. I knew I had to remain courageous, not only for my own sake but for the future of my family. My thoughts raced to Satvik's laughter, to the dreams I had for him. I couldn't let this disease take that away from us.

As Jayu wiped her tears, I reached for her hand, squeezing it tightly. "We will face this together," I assured her. The journey ahead would be long and difficult, but I felt a renewed sense of purpose. I was ready to fight, to explore every option, and to battle this cancer with everything I had.

In that moment, surrounded by uncertainty, I chose hope over despair. Together, we would navigate this dark path, hand in hand, determined to find the light at the end.

CHAPTER XIII

Preparing for the Fight

Returning home after receiving my diagnosis was a bittersweet moment. The weight of the news loomed heavy in the air, especially for Jayu. I could see the depression settling in around her like a thick fog. It was as if the vibrant light that had always been a part of her spirit had dimmed, replaced by a suffocating fear of what lay ahead. In those moments, I knew it was my turn to be the source of courage and strength.

"I know it's hard, Jayu," I said softly, trying to reach out to her. "But we can't give up. Our love and our family are what will get us through this." I hoped my words would provide a glimmer of hope, even if I felt the darkness creeping in myself.

One of the most important tasks ahead of me was telling Satvik about my condition. I wanted him to hear it from me before anyone else did, to understand it in a way that wouldn't frighten him. I took a deep breath and sat down with him.We call my son 'Kittupi' at home. "Kittupi, I need to tell you something important," I began, looking into his curious eyes.

"Appa has a disease called cancer, but it's okay. It's like having a fever, and with the right treatment, I will get better," I explained gently. I could see the confusion and concern on his face, so I continued, "If you hear someone talking about it, I want you to remember that I'm a lion, and lions are strong. You don't need to cry or be afraid."

His expression shifted from worry to understanding, and I felt a wave of relief wash over me. We were in this together, and I wanted him to feel secure, knowing his father was fighting with all his might.

As the days passed, the three of us—Jayu, Satvik, and I—began to come together as a united front. We embraced the challenges ahead, ready to face them in every way possible. I felt a renewed sense of purpose as I prepared for my first chemotherapy session. Each day brought us closer, binding us in a shared strength that fueled my determination to fight this battle.

With a heart full of love and a fierce resolve, I stepped into the unknown, ready to face whatever came my way.

CHAPTER XIV

Rising Above the Negativity

After preparing for the fight, after gathering my strength and rallying my spirit to face the battle ahead, one truth became evident: cancer is not the only enemy I would have to confront. Along with the physical pain, the medical treatments, and the endless tests, there was a psychological war to fight as well—one that involved people.

In the midst of the most trying time of my life, I encountered something that hurt even more than the chemotherapy or the hospital visits: the shocking silence from people I once considered friends, and the cold words from those who should have shown compassion. It was disheartening, to say the least, when people who were once close, who should have been there to offer a simple text or a call, were nowhere to be found. Instead, there were people asking my wife, "Will he survive, or will he die?" Those words, spoken in such a thoughtless, casual manner, felt like a slap in the face.

But here's the lesson I learned: I didn't have to let their coldness, their ignorance, or their lack of empathy affect me. I could have let those words and those actions drain my energy, but I chose not to. I chose not to mention them, not to focus on them, not to let them take up space in my mind. They had no place in my healing process.

I understand now that kindness is something that should come naturally to all human beings, yet not everyone will show it when you need it most. And that's okay. It is not your job to change them, nor is it your responsibility to explain why they should care. Their failure to show compassion does not diminish your worth, your strength, or your value. It simply reveals more about them than it does about you.

There were many moments when I could have let the disappointment consume me—when I could have focused on the void created by those who didn't show up. But I chose to rise above it. I chose to ignore the negativity and focus on the positivity. I chose to embrace the people who stood by me, the ones who offered their support, their love, and their encouragement. These were the people who truly mattered, the ones who uplifted me when I needed it most.

Ignoring the negative doesn't mean ignoring the reality of the situation. It doesn't mean pretending that the world is perfect or that everyone will act the way we hope they will. It simply means not allowing negativity to define your story. It means not giving those who seek to bring you down any more of your precious energy. It means surrounding yourself with people who help you rise, not those who keep you stuck in the mud.

So, I moved forward. I let go of the hurt, the disappointment, and the bitterness that could have easily taken root. I did not allow the people who ignored me, or the ones who asked insensitive questions, to dictate how I would live my life. I focused on the love and kindness that I was receiving from others, and I carried that with me through every treatment, every difficult day, and every moment of doubt.

If there's one thing I can tell you from my experience, it's this: do not let others' lack of support pull you into a negative space. There will always be people who disappoint you, who don't rise to the occasion when you need them most. But that's not your burden to bear. Let them go. Embrace the people who love you, who support you, and who remind you of the strength and resilience within yourself. You have the power to rise above the negativity, to choose your response, and to surround yourself with the energy that will propel you forward.

Stay positive, stay focused, and remember that you are the one who gets to decide how your story unfolds. Let kindness be your guide, and leave behind the bitterness and the doubts. They have no place in the beautiful journey ahead.

CHAPTER XV

Understanding Chemotherapy and Preparing My Mind

Before I stepped into the world of chemotherapy, I knew one thing for sure: I needed to understand what I was about to face. I didn't want to go in blind, to be caught off guard by the unknown. And so, I turned to the resources that were available to me—namely, the internet and YouTube videos. At first, I wasn't sure if I was making the right choice, but I realized that knowledge would be my ally. Understanding the process ahead of time would give me a sense of control over something that, in many ways, felt completely out of my hands.

The first step in preparing for chemotherapy was learning what it was, how it worked, and what kind of side effects I could expect. I wanted to know everything—both the good and the difficult parts. I searched for credible sources, reliable articles, and patient testimonials. There were countless stories of people who had undergone chemotherapy, each with their own journey, and I knew that hearing from those who had lived it would give me the most insight.

I started by watching YouTube videos from medical professionals and cancer survivors. These videos helped demystify the entire process. They explained how chemotherapy targets fast-growing cells, including cancer cells, but also some healthy cells, which leads to the side effects. I learned about the different types of chemotherapy drugs and what to expect with each treatment cycle. There were stories about hair loss, nausea, and the fatigue that often followed the sessions. I also heard about the moments of strength, resilience, and recovery—the stories that filled me with hope and encouraged me to press forward.

One of the most powerful lessons I took from these videos and articles was the importance of mental preparation. Chemotherapy wasn't just a physical battle. It was a mental and emotional journey as well. It was crucial for me to prepare my mind for the challenges ahead, to accept that I would have tough days and that the process wouldn't be easy. But I also learned that chemotherapy wasn't a death sentence—it was a chance, a step toward healing.

I spent time visualizing what I might feel after each session—feeling drained, perhaps overwhelmed by the side effects—but also knowing that each treatment brought me one step closer to recovery. I trained myself to focus on the positives: the fact that I was doing something about my illness, that I was taking action, and that chemotherapy was working to shrink the tumors, to give me a fighting chance at life.

To help my mind prepare even further, I also practiced affirmations. Every day, I told myself that I was strong, that I could handle whatever came my way, and that I had the power to overcome. This mental preparation gave me the confidence to walk into each session with determination. It wasn't about ignoring the reality of what chemotherapy might bring—it was about facing it with the right mindset, ready to push through the challenges.

I also reached out to others who had been through chemotherapy. Their support was invaluable. Talking to people who understood exactly what I was about to face gave me a sense of camaraderie. It reassured me that I wasn't alone in this fight. They shared tips on managing side effects, staying positive, and finding ways to stay as comfortable as possible. Most importantly, they reminded me that chemotherapy was a means to an end, not the end itself.

Preparing my mind in this way gave me a sense of readiness, of empowerment, that I would carry with me throughout the treatment. I knew that it wouldn't always be easy, but I also knew that I had the strength to handle whatever came next. Knowledge, preparation, and a positive mindset became my tools for surviving chemotherapy.

So, if you're reading this and preparing for chemotherapy yourself, know this: the more you understand, the more empowered you will feel. Don't shy away from learning about the process—take control by arming yourself with information. Talk to others who've been through it. Visualize your strength and resilience. And above all, remember that this is just one chapter in your journey—one that you will overcome with courage, determination, and an unwavering belief in your ability to heal.

CHAPTER XVI

The Courage to Face the Storm

Chemotherapy was a battle—a storm that tested my limits, but I faced it with courage. Every session felt like an intense force, an onslaught, but instead of letting it strip me away, I chose to stand firm. The poison coursing through my veins was a necessary weapon in this fight, a means to an end. Yes, the pain was searing, and no amount of morphine could dull the intensity. Yet, despite the waves of nausea that robbed me of rest and the weakness that seemed to consume my body, I knew deep down that this was the path I had to walk.

In those moments, I didn't surrender to fear. I didn't let the pain define me. I understood that this was part of the journey—part of the fight for my life. The simplest tasks became challenges, but I found strength in pushing through them, in knowing that each action, no matter how small, was a victory. Every movement was an act of defiance against the disease, a reminder that I wasn't going down without a fight.

Jayu was my unwavering source of strength through it all. She sat by me, offering quiet support that spoke volumes. Her eyes, though filled with a silent pain of their own, were filled with a strength that gave me courage. I saw her balance everything—keeping our home running, managing our son's care from afar, all while watching me battle against this unseen enemy. There were moments when I saw the tears she tried to hide, the fear she sought to mask, but she never wavered in her support. Her presence was a constant reminder that I wasn't alone in this. Even on the darkest days, when I couldn't see the light, I could feel her love and resolve surrounding me.

Our son, still unaware of the full gravity of the situation, stayed with Jayu's family. While it broke my heart to be apart from him, there was solace in knowing that he was shielded from the harsh reality of what I was going through. He could still laugh, still play, and for that, I was grateful. But even in the midst of all this, there were moments when I longed to hear his voice, to see his face, to hold him close. The ache of his absence would strike at the most unexpected times, and in those moments, I closed my eyes, held onto the memory of his laughter, and used it to fuel my strength for the next wave of suffering.

Through every session, through every painful moment, I clung to what I knew was most important: the love of my family, the strength that came from within, and the hope that I could endure whatever came next. This journey was unlike anything I had imagined. It was relentless, unforgiving, and at times, agonizing. But I never feared it. Fear had no place in this fight. Instead, I faced it with a calm resolve, knowing that each day I made it through was a step closer to healing, a step closer to being there for my loved ones once again.

I didn't just fight for myself—I fought for the love that had carried me this far. Each breath, each small victory was a testament to the unbreakable will inside me. And no matter how many times I was knocked down, I would rise again, stronger each time. With hope in my heart and the love of my family guiding me, I faced everything courageously. And I knew, deep in my bones, that I would get through it. Because I had something worth fighting for.

CHAPTER XVII

A New Chapter in My Fight for Health

As my treatment progressed, I encountered a major challenge. Caritas Hospital, where I had been receiving care, could not provide the necessary transplantation options should I require them urgently. While the news was concerning, I didn't let it overwhelm me. Instead, it ignited a sense of urgency and determination within me. I understood that the next step in my journey was crucial, and I had to make the right decision for my health.

The need to find the right hospital for my treatment became clear. After discussions with my medical team, we agreed that a change was necessary. While this wasn't an easy decision, I knew it was essential for my recovery. My health had to be the priority, and I was willing to do whatever it took to ensure I had the best care possible.

Changing hospitals was no small feat. It meant stepping out of my comfort zone and leaving behind the familiar faces and routines I had grown accustomed to, even in the midst of my illness. But I embraced the challenge with confidence. I understood that in this fight, adaptability was just as important as resilience. I wasn't going to let fear or uncertainty hold me back.

With Jayu and my mother-in-law by my side, we began researching potential hospitals, considering their specialties and the care they offered. There was no hesitation in my approach. I was focused and resolute in finding the best option for my treatment. Each call, each piece of information we gathered, brought me closer to my goal. The anxiety that initially weighed on me started to lift, replaced by a growing sense of clarity and purpose.

On the day of the transfer, I felt a combination of anticipation and confidence. I knew that this was the right decision. The journey itself felt surreal, but it also felt like a step toward a brighter future. I wasn't afraid of the unknown. I was determined to face whatever came my way. Every challenge I had already overcome had only strengthened my belief in my ability to conquer the next.

In the days that followed, as we continued reaching out to hospitals and gathering information, my confidence grew. I had made the right choice to seek out better care, and I felt more certain than ever that this move was an essential part of my healing. With each new hospital I explored, I felt the weight of uncertainty lifting, and I realized how far I had come in trusting myself and the process.

This transition marked a defining moment in my battle. It was a clear reminder that sometimes, the road to recovery requires courage and the willingness to make tough choices. I didn't just trust the process; I trusted myself. And as I moved forward, I did so with the firm belief that this change was the beginning of a new chapter—one where I would continue to fight with courage, confidence, and an unwavering commitment to my health and future.

CHAPTER XVIII

A New Hope: Discovering Rajagiri Hospital

As I continued my search for a better treatment facility, I received a recommendation for Rajagiri Hospital in Aluva from a friend and colleague. They spoke highly of Dr. Sanju Cyriac, noting his expertise and compassionate approach. The mention of this hospital sparked a flicker of hope within me, prompting me to act quickly.

Without hesitating, I dialed Dr. Sanju's number, my heart racing as I waited for the call to connect. The moment he answered, I shared my medical background and the challenges I had been facing. I also sent my medical certificates via WhatsApp for his review.

As we spoke, I felt a wave of positivity wash over me. Dr. Sanju's calm and reassuring demeanor put me at ease. He listened attentively, asking questions that showed his genuine concern for my well-being. His confidence in addressing my situation ignited a sense of trust. After reviewing my documents, he encouraged me to come to Rajagiri Hospital for further treatment.

Our conversation felt like a turning point. For the first time in a while, I was impressed not just by his professionalism but also by the empathy that came through in his voice. It was as if he understood the weight of my journey and was ready to help lighten that burden. I hung up feeling a renewed sense of hope, convinced that I had found the right place to continue my fight against cancer.

CHAPTER XIX

A Turning Point: Meeting Dr. Sanju

Arriving at Rajagiri Hospital marked the beginning of a new chapter in my journey. From the moment I stepped inside, I was enveloped in a sense of calm and professionalism that instantly put me at ease. After a short wait, I was escorted into Dr. Sanju Cyriac's office.

Dr. Sanju greeted me with warmth and genuine kindness, instantly making me feel comfortable. It felt less like a doctor-patient encounter and more like catching up with an old friend. He carefully reviewed my medical history and took the time to explain my treatment options with both clarity and compassion. His thoughtful approach gave me renewed hope, especially as he outlined a comprehensive plan that included chemotherapy and other necessary treatments tailored to my condition.

But there was one significant challenge ahead: the logistics of getting to the hospital for my treatments. Traveling from my rented house to Rajagiri Hospital was no small feat, especially considering how often I had to make the journey. The distance added another layer of complexity to an already taxing situation. Thankfully, our neighbor Raju Chettan, a kind and dependable taxi driver, helped make each trip more manageable.

The commute soon became a routine. Sometimes, my brother-in-law and wife, Jayu, would accompany me, their presence offering much-needed comfort and strength. Raju Chettan, always understanding of our circumstances, ensured our rides were as smooth and stress-free as possible.

Despite the physical and emotional toll of chemotherapy, I found myself developing a sense of camaraderie with Dr. Sanju and his team. The treatment was undeniably difficult, full of side effects and emotional ups and downs, but having a compassionate doctor by my side made all the difference.

As the weeks went by, I embraced this turning point in my journey. Each visit to Rajagiri Hospital not only brought me closer to healing but also deepened the bond with my family as we faced these challenges together. With every step forward, I felt more resilient, bolstered by the unwavering support of those around me.

CHAPTER XX

Strength Amidst the Storm

Days blurred into weeks, and weeks into months, as I endured round after round of chemotherapy. My body transformed drastically; the medications caused me to gain weight, and every strand of hair fell away, leaving me nearly unrecognizable. But despite all the physical changes, my confidence held steady. No matter how much my body changed, my spirit remained unbroken.

The journey took a heavy financial toll, with my savings quickly dwindling. Thankfully, my former company, a few colleagues, and close friends stepped in with unwavering support, reminding me that compassion was abundant even in my hardest moments. Jayu was my steadfast source of courage, grounding me every day, but I could feel the weight of her sacrifices, her strength becoming my own.

Support came from all sides of our family. My parents and my brother's family visited, bringing with them the warmth and comfort of home. Their presence lifted my spirits, and though they could only stay for a short while, they gave me the encouragement I needed to keep fighting. Jayu's parents and her brother-in-law became just as essential to our journey. My mother-in-law was like a second mother to me, her care and understanding offering me a sense of safety that kept me strong. Her quiet strength mirrored Jayu's, making me feel as though I was surrounded by a protective shield of family love.

Determined to reclaim some control over my life, I began working from home (WFH) between treatments, even on days when my body felt weak. My work gave me purpose, and each paycheck helped ease the burden of our growing medical expenses. Alongside work, I turned to writing, pouring my feelings into poems that chronicled my journey and struggles. Writing became a form of healing, a way to capture and release the emotions I couldn't always express. It reminded me that there was a part of myself that cancer could not touch.

With Jayu's unwavering love, the support of both our families, and each word I wrote, I found strength even in the harshest of times. The journey was far from over, but with each day that passed, I grew more determined to face whatever lay ahead, knowing I was not alone.

CHAPTER XXI

The Power of Positive Energy

During my treatment, one of the most profound realizations I had was how deeply the energy and attitudes of the people around me could impact my journey. As I navigated the storm of chemotherapy, I learned that not all visitors brought with them the same level of support—some brought love and light, while others brought negativity and doubt. I had to be selective about who I allowed into my space, especially during such a fragile time.

There were visitors who, despite their best intentions, unintentionally drained my energy. They came, offering their sympathies, asking questions that only fueled my fears, and speaking of worst-case scenarios. I remember one visitor who, after hearing about my treatment, asked my wife, "Do you think he's going to survive?" It stung. Not only was it an inappropriate question, but it also planted a seed of doubt. In a moment when I needed strength and courage, their words made me feel like my fight was already lost. I realized quickly that I couldn't let these moments overshadow my resolve.

I chose not to engage with these visitors for long. When they came, I smiled, nodded, and politely excused myself when necessary. I realized that I didn't owe anyone my time or energy, especially if their presence was dragging me into a pit of negativity. I wasn't going to let other people's fear dictate my journey. I had learned to protect my mind and my heart—this battle was as much mental as it was physical, and I needed to guard my thoughts carefully.

But not all visitors brought negativity. There were those who brought light, love, and laughter with them. These were the ones I welcomed with open arms. They would sit with me, not asking about the prognosis or dwelling on the difficult parts of the treatment, but instead focusing on the things that made me smile. They brought with them an energy that lifted me up. They reminded me of the world outside of the hospital room, of the joys of life, and of the dreams I still had. These people helped me feel connected to something bigger than my illness—they reminded me of what I was fighting for.

One friend in particular was a beacon of positivity. Instead of asking me about my pain or about the grim details of my treatment, they would tell funny stories, share good news, or simply talk about their life, making me feel like a person again, not just a cancer patient. Their visit was never about the illness—it was about me. It was a moment of normalcy in the middle of the chaos. I always felt energized after their visits, and their encouragement stayed with me long after they left.

The choice to focus on these positive interactions was a powerful one. I realized that my healing wasn't just about medicine or treatments—it was about surrounding myself with the right energy, the right mindset. It was about rejecting negativity and choosing courage, hope, and positivity every single day. The people who surrounded me with uplifting energy helped to restore the strength I needed to keep fighting.

I learned the importance of not letting the negative voices, no matter how well-meaning, influence my journey. I had to protect my peace. And in doing so, I gave myself the best chance to heal. I made a conscious decision to focus on the visitors who shared their positive energy and beliefs with me. I welcomed them into my space and let their good vibes fill me up.

Some may have thought I was being selective, or even distant, but I knew that this wasn't about being rude—it was about my survival. I could not afford to let fear, doubt, or negativity take root in my heart or mind. My strength came from within, and I could only feed that strength by surrounding myself with people who believed in the power of positivity.

This chapter of my journey taught me a vital lesson: Energy is contagious. The right energy—positive, hopeful, and courageous—could fuel my fight in ways no treatment could. And when I let go of the negative, I made room for the positivity that would carry me through to the other side.

CHAPTER XXII

Finding Courage Through Writing

Writing became my sanctuary, my way to process everything—the pain, the hope, the endless struggles. As I filled page after page with poetry that spoke of resilience and hardship, a thought began to form: I wanted to publish these poems. I wanted others to see the raw reality of battling cancer and perhaps find hope within my words. But another challenge surfaced—publishing required money, and between treatments and daily expenses, funds were low.

Determined not to let this dream fade, I turned to the internet, searching for ways to self-publish without incurring high costs. I spent hours on YouTube, watching tutorials on cover design and book formatting, teaching myself the skills needed to bring my words to life. It was painstaking, but each lesson was a step closer to my goal. I stumbled upon Notion Press, an online platform that allowed budding authors to publish independently, and suddenly, the dream felt within reach.

Late into the nights, after the exhaustion of each day settled, I worked on my book. Designing the cover, formatting the poems, and revising my work became a labor of love and resilience. This process, while daunting, reminded me of the strength within—proof that even in my hardest times, creativity and courage could thrive. This book wasn't just a collection of poems; it was a testament to survival, to the human spirit's unyielding determination.

During this time, I started sharing snippets of my journey on Facebook. My posts, raw and honest, unexpectedly resonated with many. As they spread, stories of my fight against cancer went viral, reaching people I never imagined. Strangers, friends, and even online media began following my updates, offering encouragement and sharing my story. Writing wasn't just healing me; it was connecting me to a community of support, reminding me I wasn't fighting alone. With each shared post and poem, I grew more determined to turn my experience into something tangible—a book that would hold my story and, hopefully, inspire others facing their own battles.

CHAPTER XXIII

Writing as a Lifeline

47

Writing became my anchor, something to hold onto in the storm of my cancer journey. Between work-from-home hours and intense treatment sessions, I devoted myself to the craft. Each line, each page, felt like another step in reclaiming my sense of purpose. After every grueling chemotherapy session, I would come home feeling drained and aching. Yet, writing brought me relief—a sanctuary where I could channel everything I was enduring into words.

Finally, I completed my first book, Raise Your Brave Wings, and took a leap of faith, listing it on Flipkart and Amazon. Slowly, people began to notice. Reviews trickled in—messages of gratitude and strength from readers who found inspiration in my words. I felt something I hadn't in a long time: excitement. The book became more than a personal achievement; it was a bridge connecting me to others facing battles of their own, forming a community of support and resilience.

My story began to attract attention beyond just my immediate circle. Publications like Manorama News, along with several magazines and online newspapers, published articles about my brave journey. They highlighted my struggles and triumphs, spreading my message of hope to a wider audience. This newfound visibility made me feel like I was not only sharing my experience but also fostering a sense of camaraderie among those who faced similar hardships.

Meanwhile, Facebook became another platform for my journey. My posts started to go viral, reaching those who needed hope, sparking conversations with readers, and even prompting personal calls from others battling their own difficulties. People began to share their stories, seeking advice, and somehow, I was helping them find their strength. Writing had transformed my pain into a lifeline—not only for me but for everyone I was reaching through my words.

As I reflected on my journey, I realized that each piece I shared, each connection I made, was a testament to the resilience we all carry within us. My story was not just mine; it belonged to all those who faced challenges and sought the light amid darkness. In that shared struggle, we found hope, healing, and a community woven together by the power of words.

CHAPTER XXIV

A Beacon of Hope

As my story began to spread, I found myself unexpectedly connected to people who were facing their own battles with cancer. They reached out, drawn by the raw honesty of my posts and the hope I tried to offer. The calls came in waves—strangers, old friends, acquaintances I hadn't spoken to in years—each one hoping for guidance, comfort, or simply someone to listen. As I heard their stories, I felt a profound responsibility not only to share my own journey but also to pass on the lessons that helped me remain resilient through it all.

One call came from a young woman in her early thirties, recently diagnosed with lymphoma. She was overwhelmed, trying to balance a demanding career with the constant fatigue and physical toll of her treatments. I could hear the exhaustion in her voice, the weight of it all. I told her to focus on what was within her control: nourishing her body, finding small moments of joy, and, most importantly, allowing herself to feel everything without the need to pretend she was okay. "Accepting your emotions and pacing yourself isn't a weakness," I reassured her. "It's survival."

Not long after, I received a call from a man, around the same age as me, who was facing an equally heavy burden—he was worried about the financial toll his treatment would take on his family. His voice was tinged with guilt as he spoke about the strain, and he wondered aloud if he should discontinue some of his therapies. I shared my own struggles, recalling the times when financial support had come from unexpected places, offering a sense of relief during dark times. "Take it one day at a time," I advised. "Help will come when you need it most, but your health has to be the priority. You can't pour from an empty cup."

But among these conversations, one call stood out—a mother reached out about her 19-year-old son, who had been diagnosed with stage two cancer. The young man, who had once been passionate about football, was now battling feelings of hopelessness. The mother explained that he was struggling to cope with the drastic changes in his life, feeling lost and depressed. She wanted me to speak with him, thinking that hearing from someone who had faced similar challenges might offer him some comfort. I agreed, and when I spoke with him, I could sense his despair.

I shared my own experiences with him—the moments of hopelessness I had faced, and how I found strength in the smallest things. "Football is still a part of you," I told him. "Your love for the game doesn't have to fade. Use it as your motivation to heal. Set small goals, whether it's practicing your skills at home or visualizing yourself back on the field." I encouraged him to embrace his passions and reminded him that it was okay to feel lost, but he didn't have to stay there. In that moment, I hoped he could feel the flicker of hope I had once struggled to find.

Then there was a call that shook me to my core—a man, 28 years old, who was grappling with the heart-wrenching decision of whether or not to tell his fiancée and her family about his diagnosis. He was afraid of how it might affect his relationship and his future. His voice trembled as he spoke about the uncertainty surrounding his marriage and life after, or even during, treatment. "What if she doesn't understand?" he asked. "What if she leaves me because of this?"

I could hear the fear in his words, the weight of the secrecy he was carrying. I took a deep breath, remembering my own struggles with vulnerability, and I shared with him the importance of honesty. "Cancer is already hard enough without carrying the burden of secrets," I said. "It's not easy, but telling her the truth will not only relieve some of your burden but also allow her to be a part of your journey. You don't have to face this alone. Relationships are built on trust, and you are not weak for needing support." I reassured him that, no matter what, his worth was not defined by his diagnosis. His fiancée would likely appreciate his openness and strength in sharing the truth, rather than being overwhelmed by fear and uncertainty.

Each of these conversations became a thread in the fabric of my own healing. In helping others navigate their struggles, I found a deeper understanding of my own journey. These moments of connection—the shared resilience, the collective strength—became my lasting purpose. I realized that my pain, my story, had grown into something much larger than myself: it had become a beacon for others. Every conversation was not only about offering hope to someone else but also about reminding myself of the courage it took to walk this path in the first place.

In each person I spoke to, I saw echoes of my own fears and strengths. Their stories mirrored mine, and in encouraging them, I found myself healing too. The shared humanity between us all—whether it was offering advice or simply listening—created a space where we could stand together, no longer isolated in our individual struggles. These connections, like a network of light, illuminated the way forward for all of us.

I will never forget the many souls who reached out to me during my treatment, and I will always be grateful for the role I played in helping others. Because of them, I knew that even in the darkest moments, I was never truly alone.

CHAPTER XXV

Quest for Knowledge

In the midst of my cancer treatment, when my body was fighting a relentless battle, I found something that kept me grounded, something that gave me a sense of purpose and direction—learning. It wasn't about the grades or certifications. It wasn't about proving anything to anyone. It was simply about giving myself something to hold onto, something that would allow me to move forward despite the overwhelming challenges.

During those long days when I could barely summon the energy to get out of bed, I made a commitment to myself: I would learn something new every day. It became a small act of defiance against the illness that had taken so much from me. No matter how difficult or exhausting the day was, no matter how much pain I felt, I would find a way to push my mind forward.

The beauty of learning is that it doesn't require perfect conditions. I didn't need to be at my best physically to open a book, watch a video, or listen to a lecture. Sometimes it was just a few minutes in between treatments, sometimes in the quiet moments after my body had been drained of energy. But even in those fleeting moments, my mind stayed active. I would dive into something new—whether it was a concept in technology, an idea in business, or a new technique to improve my personal life. It didn't matter the topic; what mattered was that I was actively engaged, giving myself something positive to focus on in the midst of everything else.

I remember feeling the heaviness of treatment and the fatigue that weighed down on me. There were days when lifting my phone to read an article felt like an impossible task. But I always told myself, "Just a little more. Just one more thing to learn today." And often, those small bits of knowledge turned into the spark of hope I needed to continue. It wasn't about mastering everything—it was about trying. The act of learning, of pushing my mind to absorb new information, gave me a sense of accomplishment, a feeling that, even if my body was struggling, my mind could still grow, still thrive.

Each day, I made an effort to learn something new, no matter how small. I found that learning wasn't just about expanding my knowledge—it was about staying connected to a life beyond the treatments, the pain, and the fear. It allowed me to tap into a deeper part of myself, to remind myself that there was more to me than just the cancer. There was a world of possibilities, and though I couldn't always engage with it physically, I could still engage with it mentally. That realization was powerful. Even though my circumstances were beyond my control, I could still control how I spent my time. And I chose to use that time to learn, to grow, and to nourish my mind.

Learning also became a way to manage the uncertainty. Cancer is a disease filled with unknowns, with days that seem endless and moments that feel overwhelmingly bleak. But in those moments, diving into something new gave me a sense of order, a sense of control. Whether it was a new skill, a deeper understanding of something I already knew, or even something I never imagined I would study, each lesson provided a small piece of stability. It wasn't just about keeping my mind distracted; it was about keeping my spirit strong.

And as the days wore on, something incredible happened—my commitment to learning not only kept my mind engaged, but it also led to an unexpected honor. In the midst of all the physical trials, I was honored with a doctorate in Information Technology. It was a recognition that felt surreal in those dark days, a tangible acknowledgment of all the time and effort I had invested in my education, even when every day seemed like a battle just to survive. The fact that I had earned such an honor, despite the challenges I faced, was a powerful testament to the strength of the human spirit. It was proof that, no matter the circumstances, there is always a way to rise.

But the honor didn't end there. Throughout my journey, I continued to learn and grow. I enrolled in various online courses through platforms like Coursera, Google, and others, covering topics ranging from IT and programming to management and leadership. Despite the difficulty of my physical condition, I committed myself to finishing those courses, gaining new skills, and obtaining certifications that boosted my confidence. Each course was a step forward, a reminder that I could keep moving, keep evolving, even in the midst of adversity.

That doctorate wasn't just an academic achievement—it was a symbol of perseverance, a reminder that knowledge is a force that can never be taken away. Even when my body was weak, my mind was strong. It proved to me that cancer could not define me, that I was still capable of growth and success in the face of adversity. It became one of the brightest moments in a difficult journey, and it reinforced my belief that learning is a tool that helps us not only survive but thrive, even in the toughest of times.

In those months, I discovered something truly remarkable: my quest for knowledge became part of my healing. It wasn't just a way to pass the time; it was a tool that kept me moving forward. Each day, as I tried to learn something new, I also learned to be patient with myself. There were days when I couldn't concentrate. There were days when my body couldn't keep up. But I never stopped trying. And each time I opened my mind to something new, no matter how small or insignificant it seemed, I was reminding myself that I was still here, still fighting, still growing.

Looking back, I can see how important that commitment to learning was. Cancer was a battle, but it was also a time of personal growth. The lessons I learned during those difficult days weren't just about the topics I studied—they were about resilience, patience, and the power of the human spirit. Even in the most difficult of circumstances, I found a way to rise. And I will carry that sense of learning, that commitment to growth, with me always, no matter what challenges lie ahead.

CHAPTER XXVI

The Blessing of Teachers

As I reflect on the people who have helped me stay strong throughout my cancer journey, I cannot forget the teachers who became more than just educators—they became my pillars of support, showing me kindness and love when I needed it the most.

One teacher who stands out in my heart is Shanthi, my class teacher during school. She was always more than just someone who taught me lessons in a classroom. Shanthi ma'am was the first to call me during my treatment, offering words of encouragement and showing concern for my well-being. Even in the toughest moments of my journey, she would reach out, checking on my health, praying for my recovery, and reminding me that I wasn't alone. Her calls became a beacon of light in the midst of darkness, and I drew strength from the fact that someone so caring was keeping me in their thoughts. Her prayers were like a shield, comforting me with every word, giving me the courage to fight when it felt like the battle was too much to bear.

What meant even more was that she didn't just call me during the hardest times. Even after my treatment, she continued to check in, offering her support and keeping me in her prayers. It wasn't just a one-time act of kindness, but a continuous outpouring of love and concern. In a world where life moves on quickly, Shanthi ma'am stood as a reminder that there are people who care, people who genuinely wish for your well-being.

Then, there was Nisha, my teacher from +1 and +2, who also made a remarkable impact on my journey. Nisha ma'am's kindness and warmth were evident long before I faced this health battle, but during my treatment, her support took on a deeper meaning. She came to visit me at home, praying for my recovery and offering a presence that gave me strength when I needed it the most. It wasn't just her prayers that made a difference, but her genuine care. When she walked into my home, it felt like a surge of positive energy filled the room. Her visit reminded me that there were people beyond my immediate family who believed in me, who were praying for me to get better, and who were hoping for my recovery just as much as I was.

These two teachers—Shanthi ma'am and Nisha ma'am—taught me more than any textbook could. They taught me the power of compassion, the importance of staying connected to one another, and the incredible healing that comes from the prayers and support of those who care. Their kindness reminded me that there are good people in the world, people who will stand by you through thick and thin, even when life is at its hardest. They showed me that healing is not just physical, but emotional and spiritual too, and sometimes, it's the strength of others' prayers and support that helps you find your own inner strength.

As I continue my journey of recovery, I carry the love and prayers of these teachers with me. Their presence in my life has been a gift, a constant reminder that even when things seem uncertain, there are people who believe in you and will stand by you no matter what.

To Shanthi ma'am, to Nisha ma'am, and to all the teachers who give more than just lessons but heart and soul—thank you. You are not just educators. You are the guiding lights, the silent warriors who give us the courage to keep going, even when the road seems impossible. Your impact goes far beyond the classroom. Your support, your prayers, and your love are etched in my heart forever.

CHAPTER XXVII

Ancy Ma'am: My Guiding Light

There are people who come into your life and, in ways you can't always explain, become more than just colleagues or friends—they become family. For me, one such person is Ancy Kuruvila, my colleague and a source of unwavering strength throughout the entire course of my treatment. I often call her "Ancy Ma'am," but to me, she is so much more. She is the elder sister I never had, a steady, nurturing presence who stood with me before my diagnosis, throughout the toughest days of my treatment, and long after it ended.

From the moment I first met Ancy, I felt a bond that transcended the usual colleague relationship. It wasn't just her professional demeanor or her kind smile; it was her innate ability to make everyone around her feel cared for, supported, and valued. Even before my treatment began, she was there—patiently listening when I shared my concerns, offering advice when I needed it, and above all, assuring me that no matter what happened, I wouldn't be alone.

But it was during the treatment that Ancy truly showed me what it meant to be a sister. In the face of my diagnosis, she didn't hesitate to step up. She became my rock—always available to listen, offer guidance, or simply offer words of encouragement when I felt overwhelmed by the challenges ahead. Whether it was checking in on me with a simple message or calling to ensure I was managing okay, her support was steadfast and constant. Ancy never once allowed me to feel like I was facing this battle alone.

Her presence was a soothing balm during some of my most difficult days. When I felt the weight of the world pressing down on me, Ancy's voice on the other end of the phone or her reassuring presence in person brought an undeniable sense of peace. She had this incredible ability to make everything seem manageable, to help me find the strength to push through each day.

But what made her support even more extraordinary was the way her entire family embraced me during this time. Ancy Ma'am's kindness extended beyond her own efforts; it was reflected in the love and care of her family. Her mother, her brothers, their wives, and even the neighbors—each one of them held me in their prayers throughout my treatment. I will never forget the warmth of those prayers, the way they wrapped around me like a blanket of hope. Their collective support became my lifeline, a reminder that I was cared for not just by Ancy, but by a whole network of people who believed in me and my strength.

Ancy's family treated me as one of their own. Her mother's gentle words and prayers were a comfort like no other, and her brothers, with their quiet yet unwavering support, made me feel like a part of their circle. Even her neighbors, who I had never met before, would reach out with messages of hope and encouragement, creating a sense of community that I didn't expect but deeply cherished.

Today, as I reflect on those days, I realize how truly blessed I was to have Ancy and her family by my side. Their kindness, love, and prayers made a world of difference in my recovery and continued to inspire me long after my treatment ended. Even now, whenever I think of them, my heart swells with gratitude.

Ancy Ma'am gave me something that goes far beyond friendship—she gave me a sense of belonging, a reminder that no matter what, I have people who will always stand by me. Her strength, love, and guidance carried me through the darkest days, and I will forever be thankful to her and her family for their unyielding support.

Through her, I learned the true meaning of family—not just those you're born with, but those who choose to stand with you, love you, and help you rise when you feel like you can't go on. I will always be grateful to Ancy, her family, and everyone who prayed for me, for without their love and care, my journey would have been infinitely harder.

Ancy Ma'am, thank you for being the sister I never had and for being my constant source of light. I will carry your kindness with me always.

CHAPTER XXVIII

The Fruits of Compassion

There are moments in life when a simple act of kindness becomes a lifeline. For me, one such gesture came from my colleague, Jiby—someone whose quiet compassion made an indelible mark on my journey through treatment.

Throughout those difficult months, when the world felt heavy and uncertain, Jiby found a way to bring light into my life, even from a distance. Every month, without fail, she arranged for a delivery of fresh fruits to my home. It was a simple yet powerful gesture: a fruit seller would show up at my door, carrying a carefully packed box of vibrant fruits—each one chosen with care, as though Jiby had handpicked them herself, just for me.

I can still remember the comfort those deliveries brought. It wasn't just the sweetness of the fruit, but the thought behind it. Each time I opened the door to receive that package, I felt a wave of warmth, knowing that someone cared for me in a way that was so tangible, so pure. In the middle of the long days of treatment, when I sometimes struggled to find the energy to smile, Jiby's kindness gave me something to look forward to. The fruit, a simple offering, carried with it her love, her support, and a reminder that I was not walking this difficult path alone.

What struck me even more was how Jiby's kindness didn't stop once the fruits had been delivered. Despite the demands of her own life, she continued to check in on me, reaching out with messages to see how I was doing. It wasn't just about sending fruit every month—it was about showing up, even in small ways, with a heart full of care.

Her friendship didn't fade away after the deliveries stopped. In fact, it grew stronger. Even now, we still stay in touch, and I consider her not just a colleague, but a friend who walked beside me in a very real way during one of the toughest times of my life.

Sometimes, it's easy to forget that kindness is not always grand gestures; often, it's the simple, thoughtful acts that leave the deepest impressions. Jiby's monthly fruit deliveries were more than just about nourishment—they were about love, about sustaining me in ways I couldn't always put into words. They were a reminder that there are angels among us, not always visible, but always present when we need them most.

As I reflect on those moments, I realize that Jiby's generosity taught me something invaluable: that the smallest acts of kindness can have the most profound impact. And even now, as we continue to stay in touch, I am reminded of the power of human connection and how it can transcend the challenges we face. Her friendship, like the fruits she sent, has nourished my soul in ways I will never forget.

CHAPTER XXIX

The Unseen Truths

Life has a way of teaching us lessons in unexpected ways, and sometimes, those lessons come from the very people we once considered close—friends, colleagues, and even those we believed would always stand by us. During my cancer journey, I experienced moments of profound disappointment that have shaped my understanding of relationships, kindness, and the true meaning of friendship.

One of the hardest lessons I learned came from someone I had always considered a brother—**my colleague** from Pune, someone who had been with me not only during my early career but also during many pivotal moments in my life. We studied together, worked together, and shared countless memories. Over the years, we built a friendship that felt unbreakable. I always wished for his success and happiness, and I always considered him a part of my family. Through good times and bad, I thought we had each other's backs. He was my best friend, and I was certain that, in return, he would always stand by me, no matter the circumstances.

However, when the news of my cancer diagnosis reached him, I was left in shock. **He never called. He never messaged.** Not once did he check in to see how I was doing. It hurt deeply. At a time when I was fighting one of the hardest battles of my life, someone I had trusted and considered a brother chose to remain silent. I thought about all the moments we had shared, the late-night talks, the plans we had for the future, and how, at one point, I had been there for him during his own struggles. And yet, in my time of need, he was absent.

It wasn't just the silence that hurt—it was the realization that people we consider close may not always be the ones who show up when it matters the most. This experience left a wound, and for a long time, I couldn't understand why he chose to distance himself. My heart ached because I had always wished for the best for him, and in return, all I got was absence when I needed support the most.

But as painful as it was, this experience gave me clarity. It taught me something essential about the nature of people and relationships. Not everyone will show up when you need them. Not everyone will extend the kindness you expect. And that's okay. It's important to recognize that not everyone has the capacity to give love, support, or empathy, and sometimes, that says more about them than it does about you.

I realized that I had been relying on someone who was not capable of being there for me in the way I needed. It was a painful truth, but it was also a lesson that helped me grow. I learned that my worth, my strength, and my ability to get through this battle did not depend on anyone else. I could no longer place my hope and expectations in others who were not willing to meet me halfway.

Instead, I chose to focus on those who did stand by me. The people who reached out, offered their prayers, sent messages of encouragement, and showed up in ways that made a difference. It was these people who reminded me of the true meaning of friendship and love. The ones who truly care will show up, no matter the distance, no matter the hardship.

Through this painful experience, I also realized that it's important to set boundaries and protect your own peace. Not everyone will be there for you, and that's something you have to accept. But don't let the absence of one person overshadow the presence of many others. People will come and go, but the strength you find in yourself, the love you receive from those who truly care, and the lessons you learn along the way will shape who you are becoming.

I'll always remember the lesson my colleague taught me—**that not everyone who you think is a friend will show up when you need them**. It was a harsh realization, but it also made me stronger, wiser, and more discerning in how I build relationships moving forward. I no longer have the luxury of expecting people to act in the way I hope or wish for. Instead, I trust my own ability to rise above, to find my inner strength, and to surround myself with people who truly value me.

To anyone going through a difficult time, whether it's cancer, loss, or any other challenge—don't be disheartened by the absence of those you thought would be there. Let that absence guide you to the ones who truly care, and to the truth that your own resilience and strength are more important than anything else. The people who truly matter will show up when it counts, and those are the people who are worth your energy and love.

In the end, the lesson was clear: **you can't always control how others treat you, but you can always control how you respond**. And in my response, I chose to rise—stronger, more self-reliant, and with a deeper understanding of the power of real, unconditional support.

CHAPTER XXX

Angels in Disguise

In the midst of the most challenging chapter of my life, I found myself enveloped by an invisible force—a circle of kindness and selflessness that lifted me when I felt the weight of the world pressing down. Though I may not remember every name, I will never forget the people who became my lifelines during those trying times. They formed an unbreakable network of support, helping me weather the storm, even on the darkest days. Their generosity arrived in many forms—whether financial help, a kind message, or a simple phone call—and each act, no matter how small, became a vital source of strength that carried me through.

Among the many who stood by me were Gobin, Ajeesh, Vishnu, Monisha, Manju, Veena, Jerom, Irene, and my mentor, Varun Sadekar Sir. These "angels" of compassion came from all corners of my life—old friends, colleagues, and even people I hadn't spoken to in years. It felt like they appeared just when I needed them most, whether through a reassuring text, an encouraging call, or an unexpected gesture that reminded me I wasn't walking this path alone.

Gobin was the first to reach out after reading my posts, offering both emotional and financial support with quiet strength and grace. Ajeesh and Vishnu, too, showed up at my rented home, bringing with them a sense of warmth and care that comforted me during some of my hardest days. Their presence was like a balm, reminding me that even in the darkest moments, there was love and friendship surrounding me.

Monisha and Manju, despite the physical distance between us, filled my days with warmth and encouragement. Their messages were a reminder of the power of true friendship. Jerom, Vishnu, and Veena carved out time from their busy lives to check on me regularly, their words of hope and positivity always grounding me, even when I felt lost. Irene, with her ever-thoughtful nature, was another pillar of support. She was always there to listen, offering a kind word or a piece of advice, and reminding me, gently but firmly, that I was never truly alone.

Then there was Varun Sadekar Sir, my mentor, whose belief in me went far beyond the professional. He became not just a guide, but a constant wellspring of wisdom and strength. His support was always balanced—practical when I needed guidance, emotional when I needed comfort, and always present when I felt most vulnerable.

But there's more—my wife's friends, whose kindness and support were an invaluable part of my journey. They stepped in as an extended family, offering help in ways I never expected. Whether it was sending homemade meals, offering comforting words, or simply being there to listen, they enveloped me in their care, providing Jayu and me with an incredible sense of peace. Their presence reminded me that I wasn't just supported by my own circle but by a wider community of love and strength. My wife's friends were not just companions to her; they became my companions too, standing by me with the same unwavering loyalty and care.

And then, there were the countless others—friends, classmates, acquaintances, and even strangers—who reached out in their own unique ways. Some shared their own struggles, others offered their prayers, but all of them gave me the strength to keep fighting. Their messages, their stories, their resilience, became a constant reminder that I was never alone in my battle. In the solidarity of strangers, I found a strength I hadn't known existed.

There were also many people who prayed for me in places of worship—churches, mosques, and temples. It was a humbling and deeply moving experience to know that people from different faiths, and from all walks of life, were sending their prayers and positive energy in my direction. One of the most touching gestures came from an old schoolmate, Nithin, who, upon hearing about my situation, arranged a special prayer service for me in his church. I will always remember that moment—how his community came together in a powerful act of faith and love. That prayer, like all the others, became a source of strength, filling my heart with a renewed sense of hope.

Perhaps some names have slipped from my memory, but angels don't need names. The collective support of this community became my lifeline, a steady reminder that even in my most isolated moments, I was never truly alone. They weren't just offering help; they were guiding me, protecting me, showing up at the most unexpected moments to lift me when I couldn't lift myself.

In the quiet moments of my recovery, I realized that the love and support I received were part of something much greater than individual acts of kindness. It was a collective resilience that transcended the struggles of one person. Their love and compassion were what allowed me to keep going, to keep believing, and to ultimately heal. Today, my family and I continue to keep these angels in our prayers, eternally grateful for the difference they made in our lives. Each prayer is a tribute to their unwavering support, a reminder that compassion knows no limits, and in our shared humanity, we find hope, healing, and strength.

Their kindness, woven into the very fabric of our lives, stands as a testament to the power of community and love. Through them, I learned that no matter how great the challenge, together we can rise above anything.

Wings of Recognition

With each passing treatment, time seemed to warp and stretch, elongating every hour until it felt like an entire day had passed. Chemotherapy took its toll in ways I hadn't fully understood before. It ravaged me physically, leaving my body drained and weak, and emotionally, it seemed to chip away at the very core of my spirit. Each treatment session was a battle, one that left me exhausted, both in body and mind. The days bled into one another, indistinguishable from the last, a blur of pain, uncertainty, and the constant hum of a ticking clock that seemed to echo louder with every moment. Yet, amidst it all, I kept going—pushing through the exhaustion and the ache. I found strength in the smallest victories, the little moments of triumph that seemed so insignificant in the grand scheme of things but meant the world to me: a smile from a loved one, a word of encouragement, a brief moment of clarity amidst the fog.

And then, out of nowhere, a flicker of light broke through the dark. My book,"**Raise Your Brave Wings**", began to gain recognition. It wasn't just an accomplishment—it was an emotional release, a recognition of the raw vulnerability I had poured into those pages. The news that I had been awarded the title of India Prime Icon by Foxclues hit me like a wave. At first, I couldn't process it. It felt unreal, like a dream that I would wake from any moment. My mind raced, overwhelmed with a tangle of pride, disbelief, and a deep, humbling sense of gratitude.

The book, **Raise Your Brave Wings**, was more than just a collection of words on paper—it was my heart laid bare, a reflection of everything I had been through. It was a symbol of resilience, not just my own, but for anyone who had faced a storm in their life. It was the culmination of years of struggle and hope, of moments when I thought I couldn't go on, but somehow found the strength to take the next step. Standing there, awarded this recognition, I couldn't help but reflect on the journey that had brought me here.

I thought back to the countless nights spent writing through waves of exhaustion, my body screaming for rest but my heart pushing me forward. I remembered the moments of doubt that had clouded my mind—wondering if I had enough to offer, questioning whether my voice mattered. The setbacks had felt endless—each failure was a harsh reminder that the path I had chosen was not an easy one. Yet, in the quietest moments of the night, I had pushed through, driven by something deeper than fear, something that whispered to me that my story was worth telling, that my journey could help others find their own courage.

Receiving the award felt like standing in the light after walking through a long, unyielding darkness. It was a powerful reminder that there was purpose in every trial, in every tear, in every painful moment. The recognition wasn't just about me—it was about the thousands of others who had battled and who would continue to fight their own wars, silently, courageously. It was a beacon, illuminating the purpose behind my suffering, a reminder that pain could be transformed into something meaningful.

As I held the title of India Prime Icon, I understood what it meant to turn pain into purpose. It was more than just an honor—it was a manifestation of everything I had fought for, everything I had endured. It was proof that the darkest hours could give birth to the brightest moments. And in that moment, standing there, I finally understood: my struggles weren't in vain. Every step, no matter how painful, had led me here, to a place where my words had the power to inspire others to soar, to rise above their own challenges, and to embrace their brave wings.

CHAPTER XXXII

A Brief Respite

As I embarked on writing my next book, the news from my latest PET scan brought an overwhelming sense of relief and joy. The reports indicated no signs of cancer, a triumph I had longed for throughout my arduous journey. Happiness enveloped our home as my wife rushed to share this incredible news with neighbors and relatives, her laughter echoing like music through the walls.

In gratitude, we visited the temple, performing rituals to thank the divine for this blessing. My heart swelled with hope, unaware that this fleeting reprieve would soon be overshadowed by an unexpected twist—within weeks, I would face a second cancer diagnosis, this time more severe than before.

Yet, even amidst the joy, an unease lingered in the back of my mind. I began experiencing severe stomach and neck pain, which grew harder to ignore. Reluctantly, I returned to the doctor, who suggested another biopsy.

The results hit me like a thunderbolt—the cancer had returned, more aggressive than before. I was reminded that life can be both a blessing and a trial. Facing this new challenge, I vowed to fight again, knowing the battle would be steeper and the stakes higher. It was a poignant reminder that hope and despair often coexist, challenging us to find strength in the darkest of times.

CHAPTER XXXIII

Embracing the Second Battle

The news of my second cancer diagnosis crashed over me like a wave of despair, sweeping away the joy I had only recently embraced. Each day felt heavier, burdened by the knowledge that I was once again entering a battle I thought I had won. I could sense the change in the atmosphere at home—my wife's smile faltered, replaced by a worry that seemed to deepen with every passing moment.

Jayu, ever my pillar of strength, fought to maintain a semblance of normalcy, yet I could see the toll it took on her. Our son, Satvik, sensed the shift too; his innocent laughter felt like a distant memory. The fear of what lay ahead haunted me, but I refused to let it consume me entirely. I reminded myself of the strength I had drawn from my previous fight, a reservoir of resilience that I could tap into once more.

The prospect of another round of chemotherapy filled me with dread, but I knew I had to face it, not just for myself but for my family. I had to be their lion again, the warrior who would protect them from despair.

In those quiet moments of reflection, I penned my emotions, pouring my heart onto the pages as I grappled with the fear of uncertainty. Writing became both my solace and my sword, allowing me to articulate the pain, frustration, and flickering hope that danced within me. I knew that if I could share my journey, perhaps it could inspire someone else facing similar darkness.

As I began the treatment again, I reminded myself that every setback was a setup for a comeback. With the unwavering support of my wife, my son's innocent love, and the lessons from my past, I steeled myself for this new battle, ready to face whatever challenges lay ahead.

77

CHAPTER XXXIV

The Fight Intensifies

As I entered Rajagiri Hospital in Aluva for my second round of treatment, the atmosphere was thick with a mix of hope and anxiety. The scent of antiseptic lingered in the air, a constant reminder of the battles fought within these walls. The hospital was a place of healing, but it also bore witness to countless struggles, each patient carrying their own story, their own fight against a relentless foe.

Dr. Sanju Cyriac, my oncologist, was a beacon of support during this tumultuous time. He approached my diagnosis not just as a doctor but as a friend. His demeanor was warm and inviting, making it easier to share my concerns. "We're in this together," he would often say, his voice reassuring. His encouragement bolstered my spirits, providing a sense of camaraderie that was vital during the grueling treatment sessions.

Dr. Vishnu, another key member of my medical team, added a different dimension to my care. He was thorough, methodical, and always had an answer for every question, no matter how trivial it seemed. His attention to detail made me feel safe, knowing that my health was in capable hands.

The hospital environment was filled with a mosaic of emotions. In waiting rooms, families clung to one another, exchanging nervous glances, sharing whispered prayers, while nurses moved gracefully between patients, offering comfort with gentle words and warm smiles. I often found myself lost in thought, observing the resilience around me. Each face told a story, some filled with hope, others with despair, yet all intertwined in a shared fight against cancer.

My treatment regimen became a routine: chemotherapy sessions punctuated by blood tests and consultations. With each session, I felt the weight of the battle grow heavier. The physical toll was more pronounced this time; fatigue seeped into my bones, and nausea was a constant companion. Yet, I clung to the support of my doctors and the camaraderie of fellow patients who shared knowing glances and words of encouragement during our overlapping journeys.

It was in this sanctuary of healing that I found strength—strength in the collective spirit of those around me, and in the unwavering support of my family. Together, we faced this challenge head-on, each day a testament to our resilience.

CHAPTER XXXV

A Voice of Strength

As the day approached for me to appear on the Kerala Can program on **Manorama TV**, a whirlwind of excitement and anxiety surged through me. The invitation, an unexpected surprise, had come as a result of the recognition I'd received from my viral Facebook posts and the impact my books had on others. The program, which focused on stories of resilience, was an extraordinary opportunity to share my own struggles with a wider audience. It felt surreal to be stepping into the public eye, particularly alongside someone like **Manju Warrier**, a beloved actress whose strength and grace had captured the hearts of millions. To be sharing this moment with her felt both humbling and overwhelming.

Arriving at the studio, I was immediately swept up in the vibrant energy of the place. The air buzzed with activity, bright lights illuminating the space while a flurry of crew members moved efficiently behind the scenes. I couldn't help but feel a thrill as I mingled with the team, who worked tirelessly to bring such inspiring content to life. But beneath that surface excitement, there was a deep, vulnerable current running through me. This wasn't just any appearance—it was a chance to share my personal journey, my raw, unfiltered story, in the hope that it might resonate with others who were facing their own battles.

When the program began, I was surprised by the honesty that flowed from me. As I stood next to Manju, I could feel the weight of my past experiences, the pain and the healing, transform into a quiet strength. We spoke about resilience, about the importance of community, and the unwavering necessity of hope when life feels insurmountable. Manju's presence beside me was a grounding force. Her encouragement and support helped amplify the message I was trying to share, and together we created a space where vulnerability was met with understanding.

As I recounted my struggle with cancer—the sleepless nights, the moments of despair, and the overwhelming sense of hopelessness that often seemed to take over—I could feel the emotion swelling within me. Yet, amid the sorrow, I also shared the moments of triumph—the small, seemingly insignificant victories that had kept me going. I spoke about the love and unwavering support of my family, and how writing had become my lifeline, allowing me to process the chaos around me. Each word I spoke seemed to strike a chord, and I could see it reflected in the faces of the audience, their eyes glistening with understanding, recognition, and perhaps even a sense of shared pain.

By the time the segment came to a close, I felt a profound sense of purpose that I hadn't expected. It wasn't just about sharing my story; it was about offering something to others—offering hope, a reminder that no matter how dire the situation, we are never truly alone. I walked out of that studio not only as a cancer fighter, but as someone who had become an advocate for resilience and hope. I realized that our struggles don't define who we are. It's not the pain or the hardship that shapes us, but how we rise from it, how we turn our pain into something powerful and meaningful. And in that moment, I understood that sharing our stories has the power to heal not just ourselves, but others who might need to hear that they, too, can rise.

CHAPTER XXXVI

Triumph in the Midst of Adversity

The chemotherapy treatments had drained me in ways I had never imagined. The fatigue was all-consuming, each day feeling like a battle just to keep going. Every cell in my body ached, every movement felt like wading through thick mud, and the heaviness in my bones seemed endless. Yet, amid this overwhelming darkness, something unexpected began to take shape—something that would ultimately mark the greatest achievements of my life.

In the midst of countless hospital visits, the never-ending treatments, and the mental and physical toll that came with fighting for my life, I found solace in the one thing that had always given me peace—writing. There were days when the pain was so intense that lifting a pen felt impossible. Yet, I wrote anyway. Even when exhaustion threatened to pull me under, and I could barely keep my eyes open, I forced myself to write. Words became my refuge, my escape, and eventually, my salvation. The pain didn't disappear, but in the quiet spaces between the words I placed on paper, it became something I could bear.

During this time, I wrote and published 5 books, each one an extension of myself, poured onto the pages with raw, unfiltered honesty. The process of creating these works became my therapy, my way of channeling all the emotions, the fears, and the hopes I carried with me. With each book, I felt a sense of purpose growing within me—these weren't just stories or lessons, they were pieces of my journey, my struggle, and my will to survive.

What I never expected, in the midst of this fight, was for these books to gain recognition in ways I had only dreamed of before. At first, it was small—comments from readers, a kind word here and there, glowing reviews from people who had connected with my words. But then, the recognition began to build, snowballing into something much larger than I could have ever imagined.

The first major acknowledgment came when I was recognized by the Indian Book of Records for having published ten books during my treatment. I can still remember that moment vividly. I was tired, still recovering from a treatment session, my body heavy and drained, when I read the message. For a brief moment, I felt a shift within me—a powerful reminder that no matter how difficult the journey, we always have the ability to redefine it. That award was not just a title; it was proof that even in the darkest times, we can still rise and create something meaningful.

Soon after, the Indian Excellency Award followed. When I received it, emotions overwhelmed me. I thought back to all the long nights spent at my desk, writing through tears, pushing through pain, wondering if my words would ever matter. To be recognized for my perseverance, for my ability to continue despite the odds, felt like validation of everything I had endured. It wasn't just about the books—it was about the strength it took to create them, about the quiet resilience that kept me moving forward when all I wanted was to rest.

The recognition didn't stop there. Foxclues magazine featured my story—how, while battling cancer, I had not only survived, but thrived, publishing multiple books during my treatment. The article focused on the heart of my mission: to show others that even in the hardest of times, we are capable of far more than we think. It filled me with gratitude, knowing my story could offer hope and encouragement to others who might be facing their own battles.

But perhaps the most surreal recognition came when Foxclues named me one of the 50 Prominent Authors of India. To be listed alongside some of the country's most respected writers felt like an impossibility—a dream that could never come true. And yet, there I was. I had written my way through the deepest pain, and somehow, my work had touched enough lives to earn this honor. That moment, standing at the intersection of pride, disbelief, and humility, was something I would never forget.

As I stood in front of the mirror, holding my awards and certificates, I couldn't help but reflect on the journey that had led me here. It had been a path of immense pain and loss, but also one of incredible growth and transformation. I had entered this battle uncertain of my future, unsure if I would even survive, and now I stood before these accomplishments—ten books published, numerous awards earned, and a sense of deep satisfaction knowing my work had touched others in meaningful ways.

In those quiet moments of recognition, I realized just how deeply intertwined pain and purpose can be. Every setback, every sleepless night, every moment of doubt had led me to this point. I had written through the pain, and in doing so, I had created something that would outlast my illness, something that would remain long after the treatments had ended. It was not just a testament to my own resilience, but to the resilience of every person who has ever fought their own battle, in whatever form it may take.

And yet, even as I celebrated these achievements, I was unaware of the next challenge that awaited me. Just as the weight of these accomplishments began to settle in, I was about to face a new test—one that would take me even further into the unknown: a bone marrow transplant. But for now, I had the strength to take it one day at a time, armed with the knowledge that I had already faced the darkest of days and emerged victorious.

CHAPTER XXXVII

The Road to Transplantation

Days morphed into weeks, and still, the symptoms clung to me like an unshakable shadow. My body, already worn from the relentless battle, was beginning to show signs of exhaustion. The fight had taken its toll, and with every ache, every tremor, every step I forced myself to take, I felt the weight of it. I returned to Rajagiri Hospital, clutching the fragile hope that the doctor would have news that would give me something to hold onto. But when Dr. Sanju Cyriac spoke, his words were heavy, each one sinking deep into my heart: a bone marrow transplant was now the next step in my journey.

The news hit me with a wave of emotions. On one hand, it was a flicker of hope—a chance to fight for my life, to reclaim what had slipped away. On the other hand, it was terrifying—a procedure full of unknowns and risks that made my stomach twist with fear. The uncertainty hung over me like an oppressive cloud, casting doubt on everything. The transplant could be the key to healing, but the fear of what could go wrong was just as overwhelming.

As I left the doctor's office, a swirl of emotions churned inside me. My mind raced, my heart pounded in my chest, and I was swallowed by a wave of fear and anxiety. Yet, amid the uncertainty, I also felt something else—a quiet, undeniable resolve. I wasn't ready to give up. I wasn't ready to let this illness define me. Jayu, my steadfast companion through every storm, stood beside me, her hand gripping mine. Her support, silent but unyielding, was a constant reminder that I was not alone in this battle.

The days that followed felt like a blur—appointments, tests, decisions. The weight of the unknown pressed down on me at every turn. But in the midst of the chaos, I found moments of clarity, moments where I could reflect on everything I had already endured. The sleepless nights, the pain that never seemed to relent, the constant cycle of treatments that had begun to feel never-ending. Yet, in those quiet moments, I discovered something profound. Something I had built within myself. Resilience. I thought of my family, their unwavering love and support, always there, like a thread weaving through the chaos. I thought of Jayu, my children, the people who had stood by me, supporting me when I couldn't stand for myself. And I knew then, I could not stop. I couldn't give in to fear. I had come too far.

As the transplant drew closer, emotions ran high. There was hope, yes, but also fear—a fear of the unknown, of what was to come. I didn't know what lay ahead, but one thing was clear: I was about to face one of the hardest battles of my life. Still, beneath the fear, there was a deep, quiet determination. I had faced darkness before, and I had emerged stronger. This transplant was just another challenge, another battle to fight. And I was ready.

With every passing day, I reminded myself of one thing: life, fragile as it is, is worth fighting for. The transplant was just another step in this journey I hadn't chosen, but one I would walk with all the courage I had left. The road ahead was unclear, the uncertainty daunting, but I knew this—one step at a time, I would take it. And I would fight every single day to make it to the other side.

CHAPTER XXXVIII

The Gift of Support

The cost of my bone marrow transplant loomed over us like a shadow, especially on days when I found myself with little to no money for chemotherapy. Yet, just when I felt the weight of the financial burden becoming unbearable, God seemed to send someone to manage it. There were moments of desperation, but each time I faced a financial hurdle, support arrived from unexpected places.

Friends and colleagues, aware of my situation, reached out to my wife to offer their assistance. Their generosity was a humbling reminder of the community surrounding us, ready to lend a hand. Former colleagues, childhood friends, and even acquaintances stepped up with unwavering kindness, providing not just financial support but emotional reinforcement as well.

Each day, as I grappled with the physical toll of cancer and chemotherapy, the knowledge of their kindness kept my spirits alive. A friend would send encouraging messages every morning, while another would offer practical financial advice to help us stretch each contribution. On one particularly challenging day, just before my chemotherapy appointment, the funds miraculously came through, ensuring that I could continue my treatment without interruption.

Through these trying times, I began to realize that this chapter of my life wasn't just about my struggle; it was a testament to the power of community, the healing force of compassion, and the understanding that, whenever needed, help would arrive.

CHAPTER XXXIX

The Day of the Transplant

The day had finally arrived. I found myself lying in the hospital bed, surrounded by white walls and the persistent hum of medical machines. It was early in the morning, and the hospital's muted ambiance carried an air of solemnity. Despite the chill in the room, I could feel a distinct warmth radiating from within—the heat of anxiety, of anticipation, and, undeniably, of hope.

Dr. Sanju Cyriac and Dr. Vishnu had thoroughly explained the procedure and the potential risks involved. Knowing the risks was daunting, but their encouragement helped steel my resolve. I was aware that this procedure would be long and painful, but I also knew it was my best chance for survival. My mind drifted back to the faces of my family: Jayu's tender yet determined gaze, my son's innocent smile, and the countless sacrifices they had both made to stand by me. In that moment, I realized this wasn't just about my own survival. I was doing this for them.

As the nurses prepared me, placing an IV in my arm and checking vitals, I could sense a mix of empathy and professionalism in their movements. They'd done this countless times, I'm sure, but they also knew the gravity of the procedure for each patient who lay in this bed. I tried to ground myself by focusing on the steady rhythm of the beeping machines, finding a strange comfort in their predictability amidst the chaos of my thoughts.

Once the transplant began, I closed my eyes and let the sensations wash over me. Each passing minute seemed to stretch into an hour. My body was wracked with waves of exhaustion, yet I was determined not to show weakness. At times, I felt the edges of my consciousness blur as fatigue took hold, but I clenched my fists and reminded myself why I was doing this.

The pain was intense, unlike anything I'd experienced before. Despite the morphine, there was a lingering ache that pulsed through every fiber of my being. It was a reminder of the battle raging within me, my body striving to accept the new cells and rebuild itself from the inside out. I thought of my son, picturing his tiny hand slipping into mine, and Jayu's unwavering strength, her presence as steady as a heartbeat. These images gave me a sense of purpose—a lifeline in the midst of the overwhelming pain.

After the transfusion, I lay there, too weak to move. The nurses and doctors checked on me frequently, their gentle touches and encouraging words helping me stay grounded. They reminded me that this was only the beginning of the healing process, but they were there, rooting for me in ways I couldn't put into words.

Hours passed, then days. In the haze of pain and exhaustion, I felt myself drifting in and out of sleep. Each morning brought a new test, a new challenge, and a new round of uncertainty. Yet, beneath the physical agony, there was a flicker of resilience. I knew I was fighting for something much bigger than myself—my family, my friends, and all those who had supported me unconditionally. And for the first time in a long time, I felt that this battle might just be one I could win.

CHAPTER XL

A Month of Isolation

The moment I was led to the sterile room, the reality of isolation truly began to sink in. It was just me—no comfort of Jayu's encouraging words, no laughter from my son to break the silence. It was a cold, clinical environment, with each hour stretching into what felt like days. The doctors and nurses who entered wore masks, their faces hidden, their voices filtered through layers of PPE. There was no familiarity, no touch of warmth. Every aspect of life that once felt grounding had vanished.

The silence became deafening. It was as if the world outside had dissolved, leaving me alone in a strange, timeless void. I missed even the smallest details of family life—the clinking of dishes, the smell of home-cooked food, the comforting weight of my son's hand in mine. Each thought of them was both a balm and a fresh wave of pain. I'd find myself whispering words of love into the empty room, hoping they'd somehow carry through the walls, reaching the people I loved.

Without access to the outside world, I had no distractions, no way to escape the thoughts that surfaced. I felt suspended between two realities: the life I had fought so hard to build, and this stark, clinical room that seemed like a distant nightmare. In these moments, loneliness took on a new meaning—it was profound, a gnawing ache in my chest that physical pain couldn't compare to.

I clung to memories as if they were a lifeline. Every time I thought of my son's laughter, or Jayu's reassuring presence, it reminded me why I was enduring this. I would imagine our future, our reunion, and the sound of life filling our home again. As hard as it was to feel hopeful, I focused on my goal to return to them whole, to resume our lives together. I wasn't just battling cancer; I was fighting to reclaim the life that had been stolen from us.

In that sterile, isolated room, I found strength I didn't know I possessed. It wasn't just a test of physical endurance; it was a test of spirit, of will, of purpose. I learned to lean into my own thoughts, to face the depths of my pain and fear without recoiling. It was as if, in isolation, I came face-to-face with my truest self—the one who would do anything to keep fighting, to hold onto the love that awaited me outside.

This month, more than any other challenge I had faced, solidified my resolve. I wasn't just fighting for my life; I was fighting for my future with them. That thought, that hope, sustained me in every moment of that isolation, reminding me that no barrier—no matter how formidable—could stand between me and my will to live.

CHAPTER XLI

Reuniting with Love

After nearly six weeks in isolation, the day finally arrived. Discharge papers in hand, I stepped out of the hospital doors, breathing in the fresh air like it was the first time. Waiting just outside was Jayu. The moment she saw me, her face softened, her eyes filled with tears she'd likely held back for months. She didn't rush to speak or ask questions; instead, we simply stood there, letting the emotions speak for themselves.

As we embraced, I could feel the weight of everything she had carried alone. Her strength, her resilience, her quiet courage had sustained our family while I was away. I could sense the relief in her touch, the quiet triumph of being reunited after what felt like an endless trial. She had faced her own battles, struggling to hold everything together in my absence, and I knew this journey had left its mark on her as well. But here we were, together again.

Each detail of her face, each gesture, felt like a reminder of what I had fought so hard to return to. We exchanged few words as we made our way home, content to sit beside one another, absorbing the quiet joy of this reunion. I glanced at her, my heart swelling with gratitude and admiration. This was more than just a reunion; it was the beginning of our healing.

Re-entering our home, I was met with familiar smells, sounds, and the warmth that had been missing from my life for so long. It felt surreal, almost as if I were walking into a dream. Jayu moved around, gently fussing over me, ensuring I was comfortable, while I simply absorbed the peace of being home. We shared quiet conversations, laughter, and moments of silence that spoke louder than words. In each moment, there was a sense of renewed hope and strength, and the bond between us felt deeper than ever.

The journey wasn't over, but the hardest part—being apart from the people I loved most—was finally behind us. I was home, with my anchor beside me, and that, in itself, was the greatest victory.

CHAPTER XLII

A Nest of Precautions

As I settled back into the rhythm of home life, a new chapter began—one marked by caution and care. The world outside was still a source of anxiety, with infections lurking in every corner. My family had transformed our home into a sanctuary, implementing precautions that became our new normal. Visitors were discouraged, and the outside world felt like a distant memory. I was isolated in a single room, but rather than feeling confined, I found solace in the love that surrounded me.

Jayu took on the role of my caregiver with grace and tenderness. She treated me like a baby, ensuring that every need was met. From the moment I woke to the gentle aroma of herbal teas she brewed for me, to the way she adjusted the blankets just so, her attention to detail made me feel cherished. There was a nurturing quality in her actions—feeding me soft foods, reminding me to take my medications, and even reading to me in the evenings. Each gesture was a reminder of the bond we shared, deepened by the trials we had faced.

Satvik, my son, stepped into a role I had never imagined he could handle at such a young age. His innocence was juxtaposed with the maturity he displayed as he helped his mother. From fetching my books to keeping me entertained with stories and jokes, he filled the room with laughter. The way he cared for me—offering to help me with everything from adjusting my pillows to simply sitting beside me—brought tears to my eyes. I felt a sense of pride wash over me; in his eyes, I saw a reflection of strength and love.

Despite the isolation, happiness flourished in our small space. My room became a cocoon, a place where my family could nurture each other amidst uncertainty. Laughter echoed through the walls, stories were shared, and love was a constant presence. Though I was cut off from the outside world, I was surrounded by warmth. Each moment with Jayu and Satvik was a reminder that, even in hardship, life could be beautiful.

I began to document these moments, capturing the little details of our days—the way Jayu's laughter filled the room, how Satvik's curiosity turned every task into an adventure, and the profound gratitude I felt for their unwavering support. In this new reality of precautions and care, I discovered a deeper appreciation for life, resilience, and the bonds that tie us together.

CHAPTER XLIII

A New Sanctuary of Hope

The doctor's voice echoed in my mind as I absorbed the news: a month of daily radiation was necessary. It was a path I had not anticipated, and as daunting as it seemed, the prospect of treatment filled me with both fear and hope. To ease the daily burden of travel to the hospital, we decided to rent a house close to Rajagiri Hospital, a surreal shift in our lives for the sake of my health.

With the help of a compassionate nurse, we found a modest, cozy home just a stone's throw from the hospital. As we settled in, a wave of mixed emotions washed over me—anxiety about the treatment ahead, gratitude for the support of my family, and a lingering sense of determination. Jayu, my wife, took charge of our new living arrangements, transforming the rented house into a sanctuary. She adorned it with familiar touches from our home—pictures of Satvik, little plants, and my favorite blankets, reminding me that love could soften even the hardest of journeys.

Every day, my brother-in-law joined us, lending his strength and presence to our small family unit. He would often share light-hearted anecdotes, lifting the weight of the impending treatment. Each morning, as I prepared for another round of radiation, I could feel the support of my family wrapping around me like a warm embrace.

The daily routine began with breakfast made by Jayu—her special herbal concoctions that she swore would boost my strength. I would sit at the table, a mix of gratitude and helplessness swirling within me. My son,

Satvik, would beam at me with the innocent joy only a child could muster, reminding me that I was still a father despite my circumstances. His laughter filled the room, a powerful antidote to the fear that sometimes threatened to creep in.

The drive to the hospital became both a ritual and a test of endurance. Each day was marked by the familiar sights of our neighborhood blending into the streets leading to the hospital. As we traveled, I would gaze out the window, observing life continuing outside, and I found solace in the thought that I was a part of that life, even as I faced my battles.

At the hospital, the staff greeted me with familiar smiles, their warmth a comforting presence amidst the starkness of clinical environments. The radiation sessions, while brief, felt monumental. Each zap was a step closer to recovery, yet it also drained me physically and emotionally. I often found myself closing my eyes, drawing strength from the memories of my family waiting for me back at the rented house.

Returning home each day, I was welcomed by the aroma of home-cooked meals and the soft chatter of my loved ones. Those moments were precious, grounding me amidst the storm of treatment. We shared stories, laughter, and an unspoken pact that we would face whatever came next together. In this cocoon of love, I realized that even the most arduous paths could lead to moments of profound joy. Despite the challenges, hope glimmered brightly in the small, everyday victories that became our life during this chapter.

CHAPTER XLIV

Homecoming

As the final rays of sunlight dipped below the horizon, we prepared to leave the rented house behind, where so many memories had been forged during my radiation treatment. The air was thick with emotions—relief, gratitude, and an underlying thread of anxiety as we set off for Kottayam, my heart racing with anticipation.

Every bump in the road felt like a marker of progress, each passing tree whispering promises of healing. Jayu sat beside me, her hand clasped tightly in mine, an anchor to the reality we were returning to—a home filled with laughter, memories, and the embrace of family. I caught glimpses of Satvik in the back seat, his eager eyes sparkling with excitement about finally being back home.

As we entered our neighborhood, familiar sights brought an overwhelming wave of nostalgia. The street we had walked countless times, the shop where we'd bought treats, and the neighbors who had waved hello—all felt like pieces of a puzzle falling back into place. But amidst the warmth of familiarity, a part of me was still apprehensive. What would our home feel like after all this time apart?

The door creaked open, and I was hit by a rush of emotions—comfort, love, and the bittersweet scent of home-cooked meals mingling in the air. As I stepped inside, it felt surreal. My eyes lingered on the photos that adorned our walls, capturing moments of joy that had become my refuge during the darkest days. Each image told a story of resilience, laughter, and love.

Satvik dashed around, exploring every corner of our home, his excitement infectious. Jayu prepared a meal, her movements graceful yet rushed, as she tried to recreate the warmth of our family dinners that had been so sorely missed. I could feel the heaviness of the last months lifting slightly; the walls of our home seemed to absorb my joy and trepidation.

In the quiet moments, however, I allowed myself to reflect on the journey that had led us here. I had faced a battle that felt insurmountable at times, yet here I was, surrounded by the people I loved most. The challenges of the past still loomed in my mind, but they were tempered by the strength I had gained through my experiences.

As the night settled in, I gathered my family in the living room. We sat together, savoring the simple pleasure of being reunited, telling stories of our days apart, laughing until our sides ached. That night, as I lay in bed, I felt a profound sense of peace wash over me. The trials had changed me, but they had also strengthened the bonds that tied us together.

Home, in all its familiar chaos and warmth, was where I found my strength. I had weathered storms and emerged on the other side, still standing, still hopeful. The journey was far from over, but with each heartbeat, I knew I had the love of my family to guide me forward.

CHAPTER XLV

The Silent Hero

In the days that followed our return home, it became evident that Jayu was not just my wife; she was the heartbeat of our family, the silent hero who bore the weight of our struggles with grace and determination. She took on the daunting task of updating my parents, friends, and colleagues about my health. Each call and message was delivered with a calmness that belied the chaos of our reality. Her soothing voice was a lifeline, bridging the gap between me and the world outside my immediate struggle.

As I lay on the couch, feeling the physical toll of my treatment, I often heard her soft laughter mingling with the tapping of her fingers on the keyboard. It was during these moments that I realized she wasn't just communicating; she was writing—capturing the essence of my journey, weaving our story into words that might one day inspire others. Sometimes, she would pause and share snippets of what she was writing, her eyes shining with a mix of hope and pride.

"I think this part would resonate with them," she'd say, reading aloud something I had shared with her in my moments of vulnerability. Even in my weakness, she found strength and a way to transform our pain into something meaningful.

Physically, I struggled day by day, my energy waning at times, and yet her resilience shone brightly. She managed my medications, ensured I ate, and kept our home running smoothly. There were days when I could barely muster the strength to lift my head, and it was during these moments that her support felt most profound. She would sit beside me, a reassuring presence, her hand resting on my arm as she read aloud from my notes or shared encouraging messages from friends who were following my journey.

Amidst the uncertainty, we found ourselves waiting for the next PET scan—an impending moment that felt like both a curse and a blessing. I often caught her lost in thought, her brow furrowed with concern. I knew she carried the weight of our future on her shoulders, grappling with the fears that loomed large in both our hearts.

"Whatever the results may be, we will face it together," she would remind me, her voice steady, but I could see the flicker of worry in her eyes. It made me realize how deeply she felt the pain of my struggle; it wasn't just mine—it was ours.

As we navigated this uncertain terrain, I grew to appreciate the unyielding bond we shared. Each update she gave about my health to our families was not just a report; it was a testament to our fight, our love, and the strength we drew from each other.

Together, we faced the days, leaning into one another, preparing for whatever came next. The PET scan loomed on the horizon, but within the storm of uncertainty, there was a warmth, a quiet assurance that no matter the outcome, we were not alone. In Jayu, I found my anchor, my unwavering support, and my greatest strength.

CHAPTER XLVI

The Waiting Room of Hope

The day of the PET scan dawned with a heaviness that settled deep in my chest. Jayu, our son Satvik, my brother-in-law, and I made our way to the hospital, the familiar halls feeling both welcoming and intimidating. With each step, the reality of the moment pressed upon us. My heart raced as we checked in, and I could feel Jayu's hand gripping mine tightly, a silent exchange of strength.

As we sat in the waiting room, I watched the clock tick agonizingly slow, each minute feeling like an eternity. Jayu sat beside me, her hands folded in prayer, whispering quiet mantras to the gods she believed would guide us through this moment. I admired her unwavering faith, even as the weight of uncertainty pressed on my shoulders. I closed my eyes and focused on her presence, trying to draw strength from her calm demeanor.

Finally, the moment arrived. A nurse called my name, and we stood up, our hands still intertwined. As we walked toward the scanning room, I could sense the anticipation and anxiety radiating between us. The scan itself was a blur—a series of bright lights and mechanical whirs—as I lay still, contemplating the potential outcomes that awaited us.

Once the scan was complete, we returned to the waiting room, but this time it felt different. The air was thick with apprehension, each second stretching longer than before. Satvik, sensing the tension, clung to Jayu's side, his innocent eyes searching for reassurance. We exchanged glances, silently communicating our fears and hopes. Jayu was still praying, her lips moving softly, her eyes closed in earnest supplication.

When the time came to meet with Dr. Sanju, we entered his cabin with mixed feelings swirling within us. I could see Jayu's fingers trembling slightly as she clutched her mangalsutra, a family heirloom that symbolized our shared strength. We sat across from the doctor, who looked up from the files with a serious expression that made my heart sink.

"Let's see the results," he said, his tone steady yet compassionate. I could feel the air thicken around us as he opened the report, and in that moment, it felt like time stood still. Jayu leaned closer to me, our shoulders brushing, and I could sense her heartbeat syncing with mine.

Dr. Sanju looked at us, his gaze filled with empathy. He began to speak, and I felt the world fade away, focusing solely on his words. With each syllable, the tension in the room seemed to escalate, every breath heavy with expectation. I could hear Satvik's soft breaths beside us, and my pulse raced, the uncertainty coursing through me like electricity.

As he revealed the results, I could see the mixture of relief and concern etched on his face. The results were in, and Jayu's quiet prayers hung in the air, holding us in a fragile embrace of hope and dread. In that moment, I realized that whatever the outcome, we had already fought a battle together—one that had forged our bond into something unbreakable. As the doctor continued to explain, I could feel Jayu's grip tighten around my hand, her love and determination surrounding us like a shield against whatever news lay ahead.

CHAPTER XLVII

A New Dawn

As Dr. Sanju began to speak, I could see a flicker of hope in his eyes that mirrored my own. "I have good news," he said, his voice steady but laced with warmth. "The PET scan results show no marks of cancer. We believe you have succeeded in this battle."

At those words, a wave of emotion crashed over me. It was as if the weight of the world had been lifted from my shoulders. I glanced at Jayu, whose eyes widened with disbelief before filling with tears of joy. We were enveloped in a moment that felt like a dream—one that I had fought so hard to achieve.

The doctor continued, outlining the next steps: monthly follow-ups, weekly blood tests, and eventually transitioning to every six months if all went well. "If you have any issues, you can always reach out for a consultation," he assured, but his voice faded into a comforting hum as I took in the gravity of the moment.

Jayu squeezed my hand tightly, her joy palpable. We exchanged glances that spoke volumes—relief, gratitude, and the shared understanding of how far we had come. Tears welled in my eyes, not from sadness, but from the overwhelming realization that we had faced a formidable foe and emerged victorious.

In that small room, filled with the scent of antiseptic and the hum of hospital machinery, we became a family reborn. I thought of all the sleepless nights, the pain, the uncertainty, and the unwavering support from those around us. Each struggle had carved out a deeper appreciation for life and love.

As we left the doctor's office, the corridors of Rajagiri Hospital felt different. They were no longer intimidating but filled with a sense of triumph. I walked hand in hand with Jayu, and for the first time in a long while, I felt light. The laughter of children echoed down the halls, and I couldn't help but smile, envisioning Satvik's joyful face and the warmth of our home awaiting us.

Later that evening, we gathered with family to celebrate the good news. Jayu shared the details of the day, her voice imbued with excitement as she recounted our journey. Laughter filled the room, echoing off the walls as we shared stories, recounting the challenges we had faced and the moments of despair that now seemed distant.

That night, as I lay in bed, I felt a profound sense of gratitude. Gratitude for my wife's unwavering support, for the medical team that had fought alongside me, and for every prayer and message of encouragement from friends, colleagues, and strangers alike. It was a reminder that hope can thrive even in the darkest times.

Though the road ahead was uncertain, I knew one thing for certain: I was ready to embrace life with open arms, to cherish every moment, and to honor the journey that had led me here. The dawn of a new chapter awaited, and I was determined to make the most of it.

CHAPTER XLVIII

A Day of Gratitude

As the first rays of sunlight filtered through the curtains, I felt a surge of hope coursing through my veins. I woke up with a sense of purpose that had been missing for so long. Today was different; it was a new beginning. I got out of bed and took a moment to gaze out of the window. The world looked brighter, more vibrant—the greens of the trees more lush, the sky a brilliant blue, and the air filled with the promise of possibilities.

Kneeling beside my bed, I closed my eyes and began my morning prayer, a ritual that had anchored me through the darkest times. "Thank you, God," I whispered, my voice shaky yet filled with gratitude. "Thank you for the strength to fight, for the support of my family, and for the gift of another day." Each word resonated within me, a reminder of my journey, the battles fought, and the victories won. I felt a deep connection to something greater than myself, a warmth that enveloped me like a comforting blanket.

After my prayers, I prepared for the day ahead, feeling the weight of uncertainty lift just a bit. I walked through the house, taking note of the small details that often went unnoticed—the scent of fresh coffee brewing in the kitchen, the sound of my son playing in his room, and the warmth of Jayu's smile as she joined me for breakfast. Every moment felt infused with a newfound appreciation.

As I sat at the table, laughter filled the room. Satvik's innocent chatter about school and his friends brought joy to my heart. It reminded me of the simple pleasures in life, the moments that truly mattered. Jayu watched him with pride, her eyes reflecting a mix of love and concern, and I could see the weight she carried for both of us. I knew she was still worried about the future, but in this moment, we were together, and that felt like enough.

After breakfast, I decided to take a walk outside, the cool morning air invigorating my spirit. With each step, I felt lighter, as if the burdens I had carried were slowly being released. I noticed the beauty of the flowers blooming, the laughter of children playing, and the sound of birds chirping—a symphony of life that resonated deeply within me. I felt a renewed sense of purpose, ready to embrace whatever lay ahead.

But there was also an undercurrent of fear. The memory of my recent battles loomed like a shadow. What if the cancer returned? What if the darkness crept back in? Those thoughts nudged at the corners of my mind, but I pushed them aside, choosing instead to focus on the present moment.

Returning home, I picked up my pen and opened my notebook, ready to write again. Words flowed effortlessly as I poured my heart onto the page, capturing the essence of my journey—the struggles, the triumphs, and the unwavering love of my family. Writing had become my therapy, a way to process my emotions and share my story with the world.

As the day unfolded, I found joy in the little things: playing games with Satvik, cooking with Jayu, and even organizing the clutter around the house. Each task became a reminder that life, despite its challenges, was a beautiful gift. I felt empowered to reclaim my life, step by step, day by day.

With the sun setting on the horizon, painting the sky with hues of orange and pink, I reflected on the day. It had been a tapestry woven with hope, fear, love, and resilience. I realized that no matter what lay ahead, I had the strength to face it. Tomorrow was another day, another opportunity to embrace life fully, and I was ready.

CHAPTER XLIX

The Strength Within

As I reflect on the past three years, a profound sense of gratitude washes over me. It feels surreal at times to think about how far I've come, from the darkest days of my treatment to now, standing strong with the gift of survival. By the grace of God, I've emerged not only as a survivor but as a beacon of hope for others who are navigating the treacherous waters of cancer. This journey, though intensely personal, has never been traveled alone. It has been paved with the unwavering love and support of my wife, Jayu, my rock, who stood by me through every hardship, and my son, whose innocent laughter has been a balm for my weary soul.

The road was anything but easy. There were moments of intense pain, fear, and doubt. There were days when I questioned if I could continue to fight. But with each setback, I unearthed a resilience I never knew existed within me. I was forced to dig deeper than I ever had before, to tap into strength that I didn't even realize I had. It wasn't just about physical endurance; it was about the will to keep going despite every obstacle.

And yet, not everyone around me was encouraging. There were people who, knowingly or unknowingly, tried to sow seeds of negativity. There were those who questioned my chances of survival, some who even told me that I might not make it. I remember their words clearly, and though they stung, I refused to let them take root. Some even seemed to revel in the darkness of my situation, feeding off the fear and uncertainty they saw in my eyes.

They tried to make me doubt, to make me question if I was strong enough to win this fight.

But here's the truth: I chose to ignore them.

I chose to focus on the voices of hope, not the ones of despair. I knew that my mind was my greatest ally, and I couldn't afford to let anyone poison my thoughts with negativity. I shut out the voices that tried to bring me down, and instead, I listened to the quiet but powerful voice inside me—the one that reminded me that I was a fighter. The one that believed, above all else, that I could overcome this. I wasn't fighting cancer just for myself; I was fighting for my family, my future, and for every person who believed in me.

In the moments when doubt crept in, I reminded myself of my strength, of the unwavering love and support that surrounded me. My parents, siblings, and friends rallied around me, offering not just their prayers but their presence—staying by my side, sitting in silence when words felt insufficient, and comforting me when the pain became too much to bear. My colleagues, some of whom I barely knew, became my cheerleaders, offering encouragement when I needed it most. Even strangers reached out, reminding me that I was not alone in this battle. Their belief in me fueled my determination to rise above despair, to keep pushing forward, and to reclaim my narrative.

Despite the heavy financial burdens looming large, I chose to focus on the blessings that emerged from this ordeal—the blessings of love, support, and community. It was during these times that I witnessed the transformative power of unity. A collective spirit that uplifted me, even when I felt downtrodden, became the foundation of my strength. Every kind word, every gesture of support, every prayer became a thread woven into the tapestry of my survival. These threads formed the fabric of my resilience and hope.

Now, as I stand at the cusp of a new chapter, I embrace the role of motivator and speaker. My story is not just about surviving cancer; it's about the power of resilience, the importance of never giving up, and the incredible strength found in the love and support of those around you. I want my journey to inspire others, to ignite a spark of hope in their hearts. Even in the darkest times, light can emerge. Even when the odds seem insurmountable, it's possible to rise.

Through it all, my son's words echo in my mind: "Appa, you are the hero, and only heroes win in the climax." Those simple words have become my mantra, instilling a fierce pride within me. I realize now that true heroism is not about being invincible or perfect. It's about the willingness to fight, to keep moving forward, no matter how hard the journey may be. It's about accepting vulnerability and celebrating small victories, knowing that each step forward is progress.

And so, I continue to fight—not just for myself, but for my family, my community, and for those who need to hear that they are not alone. I am committed to sharing my story, to inspire others to embrace their own journeys, no matter how arduous they may be. Because we all have a hero within us. We all have the strength to overcome the challenges we face.

As I close this chapter of my life, I do so with a heart full of hope and a spirit renewed. The ashes of my past have transformed into a source of inspiration, igniting my passion to reach out, to lift others, and to be the beacon of light I once needed. The future holds countless opportunities for growth, connection, and healing, and I am ready to seize them with open arms.

This story is not just mine; it is the collective narrative of strength, love, and unyielding hope. It is a true testament to the hero within us all—the hero who rises, who fights, and who, no matter what, chooses to live.

CHAPTER L

Trusting My Body

Throughout my battle with cancer, I quickly learned that my body was not just a vessel—it was both my greatest ally and my most profound teacher. At the beginning, I leaned heavily on the medical advice and treatments provided by my doctors. It was only natural; after all, they were the experts, and I believed they held the key to my healing. However, as time passed and the days blurred into each other, I began to realize something crucial: while medical treatments and professionals played a vital role in my recovery, my body had a language of its own. And learning to listen to it, to trust it, would become an essential part of my healing process.

The Importance of Listening to Your Body

Cancer and its treatments take a brutal toll on the body. The fatigue is unlike anything I had experienced before. Every movement felt like a Herculean effort, as though I was wading through thick mud. I had days where even the smallest tasks, like getting out of bed or walking to the bathroom, felt exhausting. In those moments, I learned the power of slowing down. It wasn't just about resting—it was about acknowledging when my body needed a break and when it had the strength to push forward.

There were days when I felt utterly defeated by the exhaustion, yet I knew that I couldn't allow myself to fall into complete stillness. I learned that moving, even if just a little, could keep my muscles from becoming stiff, improve my mood, and provide a sense of control amidst the chaos of treatment. A short walk, stretching my limbs while lying in bed, or even just sitting up for a while—these small actions helped me feel like I was participating in my own recovery. It was a delicate balance: knowing when to rest and when to keep moving forward.

But there were also times when I had to listen and accept that rest was necessary. Pushing myself beyond what my body could handle often led to setbacks. I learned to trust the signals my body was sending, even when they meant taking a step back. Acknowledging my limits didn't feel like failure—it felt like self-care. My body knew what it needed, and by respecting that, I found I could recover more effectively.

Understanding Discomfort vs. Pain

One of the hardest lessons I had to learn was understanding the difference between the discomfort caused by treatment and the pain that signaled something more serious. The treatments, especially chemotherapy, were inherently painful. I had days where the discomfort was intense, but I realized that much of it was just my body's response to the battle it was fighting. This kind of pain, the kind that felt like a necessary part of the process, didn't demand attention beyond the usual coping strategies.

However, there were times when pain went beyond the typical treatment-related discomfort. These were the moments when I had to pay extra attention. It's easy to become desensitized to pain after weeks of treatment, but I learned to trust my instincts. When something didn't feel right, I paid attention. I kept a mental note of symptoms, and when I was uncertain, I sought help. This level of awareness empowered me to speak up and advocate for myself, ensuring I didn't ignore something that needed medical attention.

The Mind-Body Connection

As the days wore on, I realized that listening to my body wasn't only about the physical signals—it also required an emotional and mental awareness. Cancer treatment is just as much about the mind as it is about the body. The emotional and mental toll that comes with the illness can have a profound effect on your physical health. Stress, fear, uncertainty—they manifest physically, tightening muscles, raising blood pressure, and weakening your immune system. But the reverse was also true: when I made time for calmness, when I practiced mindfulness or engaged in activities that brought me joy, my body seemed to respond better to the treatments.

In the midst of all the chaos, I began practicing mindfulness—simple exercises that allowed me to center myself, focus on my breathing, and manage stress. I found that even a few minutes of meditation or breathing exercises could lower my heart rate, relax my muscles, and create a sense of peace in my mind. This small act of self-care helped me stay grounded and helped my body respond more effectively to the treatments I was undergoing.

The Power of Self-Care

As my journey continued, I realized the true importance of self-care. Self-care wasn't just about indulgence or pampering—it was about nurturing both my body and mind in ways that would support my healing process. In the midst of chemotherapy and fatigue, I began prioritizing simple things: staying hydrated, eating nourishing foods, and making sure I got enough rest. These acts of self-care didn't seem extraordinary, but they were essential. How I treated my body outside of the medical treatments directly affected how I felt during them.

Good nutrition became a cornerstone of my recovery. I learned that what I put into my body had the power to help it heal. Healthy meals provided me with more energy, boosted my mood, and strengthened my immune system. It was a small but meaningful way I could take control of my health, even when it felt like cancer was in control. Similarly, sleep became my best friend. The body heals best when it's at rest, and so I made sure I allowed myself the time to sleep, even if it meant napping throughout the day. Rest wasn't a luxury—it was a necessity.

Trusting Your Inner Wisdom

Cancer treatment is full of uncertainty. There are days when nothing feels predictable—when you don't know how your body will react, what the next step in your treatment will be, or how you'll make it through. During these times, I leaned into my own intuition. I learned to trust my instincts when it came to my body's needs. Whether it was a quiet day of rest, a desire to move, or a sudden need for emotional support, my body had a way of guiding me toward what I needed to feel better, both physically and emotionally.

I learned not to second-guess myself, especially when it came to making decisions about my care. If something felt wrong, I asked questions. If a treatment didn't feel right, I sought a second opinion. Listening to my body, and trusting my inner wisdom, became one of the most empowering aspects of my healing process.

The Journey of Trust

As I look back on my journey, I see how integral this connection with my body has been to my survival. Cancer didn't just affect me physically—it changed the way I viewed myself and my health. In the beginning, I felt out of control, like my body had betrayed me. But over time, I began to understand that my body was not the enemy. It was a partner in my healing, a partner that could guide me, teach me, and help me recover.

Trusting my body wasn't always easy. It required patience, awareness, and a willingness to listen deeply. But in the end, it was this trust—this bond between mind and body—that carried me through the hardest moments. By tuning into the signals my body sent, respecting its limits, and giving it the care it needed, I was able to reclaim a sense of control and power during a time when so much of my life felt uncertain.

Cancer is a fight, there's no doubt about it. But the journey is not just about surviving the disease—it's about finding ways to thrive, even when it feels impossible. My body, with all its frailties and resilience, taught me that. It is not just a vessel for treatment; it is a companion on the path to healing, and by trusting it, I found my strength.

CHAPTER LI

Power of a Hobby

Cancer is a relentless battle. From the moment the diagnosis is made, it feels like your world is turned upside down. The physical and emotional toll is immense, and there are days when the weight of it all seems unbearable. The treatments, the exhaustion, the uncertainty—they drain you in ways you never thought possible. But amidst this overwhelming storm, I found something that kept me grounded, something that provided a sense of normalcy and comfort—my love for reading.

At first, it seemed like a distant dream. On my worst days, even the thought of holding a book or focusing on a page felt too much. But in the quieter moments, when the treatments were on pause, when the pain was bearable, I would reach for a book. It didn't matter what kind—fiction, self-help, biographies, or even poetry. What mattered was the escape it provided. Reading became my refuge, my therapy, my way of reclaiming a piece of peace in the midst of chaos.

Reading allowed me to leave behind the sterile smell of hospital rooms, the hum of chemotherapy machines, and the heaviness of my own body that felt foreign to me. It transported me to different worlds, made me laugh, made me cry, and reminded me that life, in all its complexity, was still beautiful. Sometimes, I needed a break from my own story, and books gave me that. They reminded me that I was not defined by my illness. I was still a person with interests, dreams, and thoughts far beyond cancer.

One of the first books I picked up during my treatment was a novel I had been meaning to read for years. As I struggled to focus on the words through the fog of fatigue and pain, I reminded myself that it didn't matter if I read a page or a chapter a day. The goal wasn't to finish it quickly—it was to let the process of reading bring me peace. Slowly but surely, the pages began to turn, and with each word, I felt a little more like myself again. It wasn't about escaping reality, but about finding small moments of joy, hope, and calm amidst the overwhelming storm of cancer.

In the quiet hours between treatments, when the world seemed to move too quickly, books became my way of slowing things down. I would curl up with a good novel, or at times, a self-help book that gave me strategies for managing the emotional rollercoaster of cancer. These books weren't just distractions—they were lifelines. They offered wisdom and perspective, reminding me that I wasn't the only one to face adversity, that others before me had fought battles and come out stronger.

As I read, I began to notice something shifting inside me. A sense of purpose began to return. Writing and reading were things I had loved before, but cancer had made me question if I would ever have the energy or time for them again. What I realized, however, was that they didn't require perfect health to appreciate. They didn't ask for anything other than my attention and willingness to engage. And in return, they gave me something invaluable—hope.

Reading also gave me a deeper understanding of myself. Books provided an avenue for reflection, for processing the emotions I hadn't yet fully understood. In the characters I encountered, I saw glimpses of my own strength, my own vulnerability, and my own growth. I learned new ways of coping, new ways of thinking, and new ways of being. It felt like I was becoming more than just someone who had cancer; I was someone who was learning, evolving, and healing in other ways.

I found particular solace in stories of survival and perseverance. Reading about people who had gone through their own struggles—whether they were battling illness, personal loss, or hardship—reminded me that resilience is a human quality. We all have the ability to rise above our challenges, to find meaning in the suffering, and to move forward with courage. These books weren't just about escaping; they were about understanding the power of the human spirit, and how even in the darkest times, there's a way to hold onto hope.

Eventually, I began to write as well. My thoughts, my emotions, my journey all flowed onto the pages, in the same way that I had once read. Writing became a cathartic process for me, and I found myself healing in ways I hadn't expected. Putting my feelings into words not only helped me understand my own struggles, but it also gave me a way to connect with others. It was my way of sharing my story, my way of saying, "I am still here, and I am still fighting."

But whether it was reading or writing, the key was finding something I loved—something that helped me keep a sense of identity outside of the illness. Cancer may have changed my life, but it didn't have to take away the things that made me feel whole. A hobby, a passion, a creative outlet—these were the things that kept me going when everything else felt out of control. They were my constant, my anchor.

In the end, it wasn't just about surviving cancer. It was about living fully, even in the midst of treatment. It was about holding onto the things that mattered to me, that made me feel connected to life, to joy, to hope. And for me, reading and writing were the lifelines that kept me afloat when the tide of illness tried to pull me under.

If there's one piece of advice I would give to anyone fighting cancer, it's this: find a hobby, find a passion, find something that fills you with purpose and joy. It could be reading, painting, knitting, gardening—anything that brings you peace. Let it be your escape, your sanctuary, your reminder that life still has beauty, even in the midst of hardship. It won't make the pain go away, but it will make the journey a little easier to bear.

CHAPTER LII

Resilience

Cancer treatment is an unpredictable journey—one that tests not only your body but also your mind and spirit. There are days when it feels like progress is being made, but then there are the inevitable setbacks—moments when things don't go as planned, when hope seems distant, or when the fatigue feels overwhelming. But one of the most important lessons I've learned throughout this process is that setbacks are not the end of the story. In fact, they often serve as the foundation for comebacks.

During my treatment, I faced numerous setbacks. Sometimes they were physical: a delayed treatment due to how my body was responding, or complications arising unexpectedly. Other times, the setbacks were emotional. There were moments when the weight of the situation felt unbearable, or when fear and uncertainty crept in. But in each of these moments, I reminded myself that setbacks were not to be feared; they were opportunities in disguise. They were chances to pause, reassess, and come back with even more determination.

The first step in navigating setbacks is accepting that they are a part of the process. No one's cancer journey is smooth, and no matter how much we prepare, things won't always go as planned. Whether it's a physical reaction to treatment, an emotional low, or a delay in progress, it's okay to feel disappointed or frustrated. I know I did. But over time, I realized that setbacks do not define who I am—they refine me. They offer a chance to reset, to adjust my course, and to continue moving forward with more clarity and strength.

It's essential to remember that setbacks don't have to signal defeat. They are part of the learning process, a natural element of the path to healing. Every time something went wrong, it was an opportunity to discover new resilience within myself, to build strength where I thought I had none left. Resilience, I learned, is the key to overcoming setbacks. It is the ability to bounce back no matter how many times you are knocked down.

The power of resilience is often revealed in the toughest moments. It is in those times of struggle that we find out what we are really made of. With every setback, I discovered new layers of my strength. Sometimes that strength was physical—getting out of bed, taking a short walk when I didn't think I could. Other times it was emotional—allowing myself to cry, to feel the pain, but then finding the courage to rise again.

What I learned is that setbacks are not failures, but rather opportunities to grow. Instead of seeing them as obstacles, I began to view them as lessons. They were chances to adjust my approach, to reconsider my mindset, and to continue moving forward with more knowledge and experience.

When setbacks occur, it's easy to become consumed by them. They can cloud your vision and make it difficult to focus on the bigger picture. However, it is important to remember that setbacks are temporary, but your long-term goals remain constant. Whether those goals involve completing treatment, regaining your health, or finding peace of mind, they are still within reach. It is crucial to remind yourself of the bigger picture when things go wrong.

Staying focused on the long-term goal helps keep setbacks in perspective. While setbacks can feel overwhelming in the moment, they are just a small part of a much larger journey. With each setback, I found a renewed sense of purpose, a deeper desire to push forward and reach the finish line. Reminding myself of my goal gave me the strength to continue, even when I wanted to quit.

Throughout my treatment, I also found the importance of having a support system. Setbacks can be emotionally draining, but they are easier to face with the help of others. Family, friends, and my medical team played a crucial role in helping me regain perspective. They reminded me of my strength and purpose, and they provided the emotional support I needed during my hardest days. It was through their encouragement that I found the courage to continue my journey.

Having people to lean on doesn't make you weak; it strengthens you. Asking for help, whether it's emotional support or assistance with everyday tasks, can make all the difference in your ability to cope with setbacks. It's important to remember that you don't have to go through this alone.

One of the most powerful things I learned was how to turn setbacks into fuel for motivation. Every time something didn't go as planned, I chose to channel my frustration, fear, and sadness into determination. I didn't let the setbacks drain me; I used them to fuel my drive to keep going. When things were at their hardest, I reminded myself why I was fighting, and I used that reason to push forward with even more strength and resilience.

Refusing to stay down was a key part of overcoming setbacks. They are inevitable, but they are also temporary. With each challenge, I reminded myself that I was one step closer to my goal, and that each setback was just another part of the journey toward recovery.

Setbacks are a natural part of the cancer treatment process, but they don't have to define your journey. Instead, they can be the things that propel you forward, that help you grow stronger, and that remind you of your own resilience. Every time you face a setback, take a moment to reflect, to learn, and then use it to fuel your comeback. Your ultimate goal is still within reach, and every setback is just a stepping stone toward your victory. Keep going, because with every setback, you are one step closer to healing.

CHAPTER LIII

Surround Yourself with Positivity

As you navigate through cancer treatment, the people around you play a crucial role in your emotional well-being. One of the most important lessons I learned during my journey was the impact that the energy of others can have on your mental state. It's easy to get bogged down by negative thoughts, especially when the road ahead seems uncertain. That's why surrounding yourself with positive people and focusing on speaking only positive things can make all the difference in how you experience your healing process.

During my treatment, I realized that I had to be mindful of the people I allowed into my space. Negative energy, even from well-meaning friends or family members, can sometimes add unnecessary stress. It wasn't that I wanted to shut people out, but I found that the more I surrounded myself with individuals who uplifted and encouraged me, the better I felt emotionally and physically. Positive people radiate optimism, and their energy can be contagious. They remind you that there is always hope, even on the darkest days.

I made it a point to spend time with those who spoke words of encouragement, who celebrated even the smallest victories with me, and who shared in the joy of each day I made it through treatment. Their optimism helped me keep going, especially when I felt tired or discouraged. They were the ones who reminded me of my strength, even when I couldn't see it myself.

It's just as important to be conscious of what you say to yourself and others. During treatment, I learned that speaking positively can influence your mindset and even your body's response to healing. Instead of focusing on fears or doubts, I chose to speak words of hope and strength. Every time I found myself thinking negatively, I consciously redirected my thoughts to affirmations of recovery, strength, and resilience.

It wasn't always easy, but I quickly noticed how much better I felt when I chose to speak positively. Not only did it help me manage the emotional stress, but it also helped me maintain a more hopeful outlook. Even on difficult days, I repeated to myself, "I am strong," "I am healing," and "This too shall pass." These small, positive affirmations helped shift my mindset, and eventually, my body began to reflect that shift in my attitude.

By surrounding yourself with positive people and speaking positively about your treatment and recovery, you're creating a supportive environment that encourages healing. Positivity doesn't ignore the challenges you face—it acknowledges them and chooses to focus on the strength, progress, and hope that still exists, even in the most difficult moments.

It's easy to fall into negative thinking or to seek out stories of failure, but when you focus on the good, on the small victories, and on the people who lift you up, you strengthen your ability to heal. You also set a powerful example for others, showing them how to face adversity with grace, optimism, and courage.

Surround yourself with people who inspire you, and commit to speaking positive, affirming words about your journey. In doing so, you'll create a space where hope can flourish, and healing can truly begin.

CHAPTER LIV

Holding On to Hope

Cancer treatment is a relentless journey, one that often feels like an endless battle. There are days when the pain seems unbearable, when exhaustion weighs heavily, and when the fear of the unknown looms large. On these days, it may seem impossible to find hope. But it is in these very moments of darkness that hope becomes your greatest ally.

I've walked through many difficult days during my cancer treatment. There were times when the pain was overwhelming, when the uncertainty about my future felt suffocating, and when I questioned whether I had the strength to continue. But even on the hardest days, I chose to hold onto hope—because hope is the light that guides you through the darkest hours.

When everything seems overwhelming, it's easy to get lost in the magnitude of the situation. I learned that one of the most effective ways to keep hope alive is to focus on the small, seemingly insignificant moments that bring light into your life. Whether it's a brief moment of laughter, a comforting word from a loved one, or simply watching the sunrise, these small moments are powerful reminders that there is still beauty in the world, even amidst the pain.

On the toughest days, I focused on these small victories—getting out of bed, eating a meal, or having a good conversation. These moments may have seemed small, but they were proof that hope was still alive, and that I was moving forward, step by step. Finding joy in the present was also essential. It's easy to get lost in the past or worry about the future, but focusing on today, even if it's just for a few minutes, can help to keep hope alive. Those moments of peace and gratitude built a foundation for my hope.

When everything felt uncertain, I often turned to visualization as a way to keep hope alive. I imagined myself well again, healthy, and full of energy. I pictured myself on the other side of this battle, enjoying time with my family, achieving my goals, and living my life to the fullest. Visualizing the future I wanted gave me the strength to push through the hardest days. I closed my eyes and pictured a future where I had overcome this challenge, living a vibrant, healthy life—doing the things I love, spending time with those who matter most, and achieving my dreams. That vision helped provide the motivation to keep going, even when it felt difficult.

Faith, too, became a powerful tool in keeping hope alive. Whether you find strength in religion, spirituality, or personal belief, faith can help you through the hardest days. During my treatment, I leaned into my faith, which gave me the strength to persevere. It reminded me that I wasn't fighting this battle alone. When everything else felt uncertain, my faith provided solid ground beneath my feet, assuring me that hope was never truly lost.

Cancer is a difficult, often painful journey, but there is always light at the end of the tunnel. It's important to remember that while the days may be hard, they are not permanent. Healing, recovery, and brighter days lie ahead. I held on to the belief that I would emerge from this stronger and more resilient. And I can tell you now: the light is real. It may feel distant at times, but it is always there, waiting for you to reach it.

Every day you get through is a victory. Celebrate your strength, even when the journey feels long. Your resilience, courage, and determination are your greatest tools for keeping hope alive. Keep moving forward, and trust that you have the strength within you to overcome whatever comes your way. The journey may be tough, but hope will always light the way.

CHAPTER LV

Trust Your Treatment

Cancer treatment is challenging, and it's only natural to feel overwhelmed by the uncertainty that comes with the journey. However, one of the most important things I learned during my experience is the need to maintain a positive mindset and avoid falling into the trap of negativity. It's easy to be influenced by others' stories—especially the ones that are filled with fear, loss, and failure. But it's crucial to remember that everyone's journey is different, and your path doesn't have to mirror anyone else's.

Throughout my treatment, I found that hearing about others' struggles could sometimes bring me down. While it's important to acknowledge and empathize with others, constantly reading about treatment failures, complications, or tragic outcomes only serves to fuel fear and uncertainty. It can make you doubt the effectiveness of your own treatment and put unnecessary stress on your mind and body. Remember, the stories you read are not your story. Just because someone else faced a setback or didn't recover doesn't mean the same will happen to you. Focus on your own healing and trust that your body, in combination with the care you receive, is doing the best it can.

It's equally important to be cautious of false treatments and unverified advice. The world is full of well-meaning but misleading information, particularly when it comes to alternative treatments like ayurvedic remedies or miracle cures. You'll find advertisements for "cancer cures" that are not supported by science, and promises of quick fixes that prey on your fear and vulnerability. It's easy to get tempted, especially when you're looking for anything that might offer hope. But the truth is, these fake treatments can often delay proper care and may even worsen your condition.

When you trust in the treatment prescribed by your healthcare team, you're taking the most reliable route toward recovery. Medical treatments, while tough and sometimes painful, are backed by years of research, clinical trials, and evidence that show they can be life-saving. Stay committed to your treatment plan and work with your doctors, as they are the experts. Your treatment, your doctors, and your own belief in the process will be your greatest allies.

During my own treatment, I focused on staying informed through trustworthy sources, leaning on my doctors for advice, and blocking out the noise of negativity. I learned to tune out anything that threatened my sense of hope. I stopped reading negative stories that left me with more fear than understanding. Instead, I focused on the small positive steps I could take every day to support my treatment and my health.

Believing in your treatment and maintaining a positive outlook isn't just about ignoring the challenges of cancer. It's about understanding that you have a team of experts guiding you, and that by staying hopeful, you're allowing your body to heal with the best possible chance for success. Negativity can only hold you back, while positivity and belief in your treatment can propel you forward, step by step, toward recovery.

Don't let fear or false promises deter you from the right path. Trust in the science, trust in your treatment, and trust in your own strength.

CHAPTER LVI

The Power of Forgiveness

Cancer treatment is not just a physical battle; it's an emotional and spiritual one as well. When I was diagnosed, I didn't just have to fight the disease—I had to confront a lot of internal struggles, too. I realized early on that emotional burdens like anger, guilt, regret, and resentment could weigh me down just as much as the physical challenges of cancer treatment. For a long time, I carried a lot of negative emotions—toward the illness, myself, and even others in my life. These emotions, while understandable, had a profound impact on my healing.

But one of the most powerful lessons I learned on this journey is that forgiveness can be a vital part of recovery. Letting go of the emotional weight I was carrying was just as important as the medical treatments I was undergoing. In this chapter, I want to share how forgiveness—both for others and for myself—helped me heal, move forward, and find peace during my cancer treatment and recovery.

1. What Forgiveness Meant for Me During Cancer Treatment

For me, forgiveness was not about excusing anyone's actions or pretending everything was fine when it wasn't. It wasn't about forgetting the pain or the fear I had gone through. Forgiveness was about giving myself permission to release the anger, guilt, and frustration I had been holding on to. I realized that my emotional state was directly tied to my healing. I couldn't afford to keep carrying around that weight if I wanted to give my body the best chance to recover.

In the midst of cancer treatment, I understood that forgiveness was a tool for my own healing. It was about choosing to let go of negative emotions and finding space for peace, even when the world around me seemed chaotic. Forgiveness gave me the freedom to stop being controlled by anger or regret, so I could focus on what mattered most: my health, my well-being, and my future.

2. Forgiving Others: Letting Go of Resentment

Like many cancer patients, I found myself feeling hurt by the way some people reacted to my diagnosis. Some of my friends and family didn't know how to support me. Others said the wrong thing or distanced themselves in a way that made me feel more alone than I already did. It would have been easy to hold on to resentment, but I quickly realized that doing so would only keep me stuck in a negative place.

Forgiving others wasn't about excusing their actions—it was about freeing myself. Holding on to anger and resentment wasn't going to change anything; it was only going to continue to hurt me. I had to let go of those feelings, not for them, but for me. In choosing forgiveness, I allowed myself to heal emotionally, and that emotional healing gave my body the strength it needed to continue fighting.

3. Forgiving Myself: Releasing Guilt

One of the hardest parts of my journey was the guilt I carried. I often found myself blaming myself for things I couldn't control. I wondered if I could have prevented my cancer somehow—if I had eaten better, exercised more, or been more careful. I felt guilty for the toll my illness took on my loved ones, too. I hated seeing the worry in their eyes.

But eventually, I realized that holding on to guilt was only making my situation worse. Cancer doesn't work that way—it's not about something you could have avoided. I had to forgive myself for the things I couldn't change. I had to accept that I was doing the best I could with the information and resources available to me. Letting go of that guilt allowed me to focus on healing, rather than on the past.

4. The Connection Between Forgiveness and Healing

I soon came to understand that emotional stress could have a real impact on my physical health. When I was angry or burdened with guilt, it felt like my body was carrying extra weight. My immune system, which needed all the strength it could muster to fight the cancer, was compromised by these negative emotions. But when I started forgiving myself and others, I felt lighter—physically and emotionally.

Forgiveness didn't just free my heart; it also helped my body. The less stress and anger I carried, the more energy my body had for recovery. I began to notice a shift—not just in my emotional state, but also in how my body responded to treatment. I felt more hopeful and connected to my healing process.

5. Compassion and Forgiveness: Acknowledging Our Shared Humanity

During my treatment, I realized that everyone around me was also struggling in their own way. My family, my friends, even my healthcare team—everyone was doing their best with the knowledge and tools they had. As I went through this journey, I learned to approach others with compassion, understanding that they weren't perfect, just as I wasn't. Compassion became a key part of my healing process.

By forgiving others, I allowed space for compassion. I could let go of the things that bothered me and focus on supporting my loved ones as they supported me. It became clear that forgiveness wasn't just about releasing negative emotions—it was also about cultivating kindness, both for others and for myself.

6. The Process of Forgiveness: Taking It One Day at a Time

Forgiveness isn't a one-time event. It's a process that unfolds gradually. Some days were easier than others. Some days, the anger or the guilt would resurface, but I learned to recognize those feelings for what they were—temporary emotions that didn't need to control me. I had to practice forgiveness daily, releasing the weight of resentment or regret each time it tried to take hold.

The more I practiced forgiveness, the easier it became to let go of those emotions. It became a routine of choosing peace, over and over again. And with that practice, I noticed a real shift in how I felt—not just emotionally, but physically. The more I forgave, the more room there was for healing.

7. Forgiving the Past: Letting Go of What I Can't Change

I found myself looking back at the past during my cancer treatment, wondering what I could have done differently. I realized that the past was just that—the past. I couldn't change what had already happened, and holding on to regrets was only preventing me from moving forward.

I had to make peace with the past—accept it as part of my journey—and let it go. Holding on to what I couldn't change was like holding on to a burden I didn't need to carry anymore. Forgiving the past freed me to focus on the present, on my treatment, and on what I could do moving forward to support my health and recovery.

8. Forgiveness in Relationships: Strengthening Bonds Through Understanding

During treatment, I had moments where I felt isolated, even though I was surrounded by people who loved me. Sometimes, the fear and uncertainty of cancer made it difficult to communicate, and misunderstandings occurred. But forgiveness helped me to reconnect with my loved ones. It helped me realize that no one had all the answers, and we were all just doing the best we could.

Forgiving those who may have unintentionally hurt me created space for healing in my relationships. I stopped expecting perfection from others and learned to appreciate the support I had, even if it wasn't always in the way I expected. In forgiving, I was able to strengthen the bonds that meant the most to me.

9. The Spiritual Aspect of Forgiveness

Cancer treatment brought me closer to my spiritual beliefs. I leaned on my faith to help me through the toughest moments, and I found that forgiveness was an essential part of that journey. Whether it was prayer, meditation, or quiet reflection, spirituality gave me the strength to forgive—both myself and others.

Through my spiritual practice, I realized that forgiveness was a powerful form of self-care. It wasn't just about healing emotionally—it was also about nurturing my soul. In forgiving, I allowed peace to flow into my life, creating the space for both emotional and physical healing.

10. Forgiving the Unknown: Surrendering to the Journey

Cancer treatment is full of uncertainty. You never know how your body will respond, how long the journey will last, or what the future holds. I had to learn to forgive the unknown and accept that I couldn't control everything. Letting go of the need for certainty allowed me to focus on what I could control—my mindset, my attitude, and my response to the challenges I faced.

Surrendering to the uncertainty of cancer treatment wasn't easy, but it was liberating. In doing so, I found peace and strength. I realized that, though I couldn't control everything, I could choose how I responded—and I chose forgiveness and peace.

11. The Freedom of Forgiveness

Through my treatment, I discovered that forgiveness is freedom. It wasn't just an emotional release—it was a form of liberation. Every time I forgave, I felt freer, lighter, and more able to focus on what really mattered. The more I forgave, the more my healing accelerated. Forgiveness gave me the freedom to move forward with my treatment, to heal, and to embrace the future.

12. Forgiveness: A Key to My Healing

The power of forgiveness was a cornerstone of my healing journey. It was one of the most important tools I used, alongside my medical treatment, to recover physically, emotionally, and spiritually. Forgiveness allowed me to release the emotional weight that could have held me back, and it opened the door for true healing to take place.

Choosing forgiveness was choosing peace. It was choosing the power to move forward. And as I look back on my cancer journey, I realize that forgiveness was not just a part of my recovery—it was the key to it.

CHAPTER LVII

The Power of Strength

Cancer treatment is one of the most physically and emotionally challenging experiences a person can go through. But in the midst of pain, uncertainty, and fear, I discovered something extraordinary within myself—strength. Strength isn't just about being physically powerful; it's about mental resilience, emotional endurance, and the ability to keep moving forward when everything inside you wants to give up. Through my battle with cancer, I learned that strength is not something you are born with; it is something you cultivate within yourself through every struggle, every setback, and every small victory.

This chapter is about the power of strength—how I found it, how it carried me through my treatment, and how it continues to be the force that drives my recovery.

1. Strength Comes From Within

When I was first diagnosed with cancer, I had no idea what I was in for. The fear, the uncertainty, the sheer weight of the unknown—these things were enough to make anyone crumble. At first, I thought strength was something external. I looked at my doctors, my family, my friends, and thought, "They are strong. I need to be strong like them." But as I began the treatment journey, I realized that true strength comes from within. It's not about comparing yourself to others; it's about finding what you are capable of when you dig deep and look inside.

The first time I truly felt my strength was when I made the decision to face my diagnosis head-on. I realized that

I could not control the disease, but I could control how I responded to it. In that moment, I understood that strength isn't about never feeling fear—it's about continuing to move forward despite the fear.

2. Strength in Resilience

One of the most important lessons I learned during my cancer journey is that strength is directly tied to resilience—the ability to bounce back after setbacks. During treatment, I faced numerous obstacles. There were days when I couldn't get out of bed, when the side effects from chemotherapy were unbearable, and when I felt like I was losing my fight. But in those moments, I chose to be resilient. I chose to keep going, even when it felt impossible.

Resilience is not about avoiding pain or difficulty; it's about enduring it, learning from it, and becoming stronger in the process. Every time I faced a setback—whether it was a complication, a failed treatment, or a day of feeling low—I reminded myself that this was just one part of my journey. I was not defined by these challenges. I was defined by my ability to get back up and keep fighting.

3. Physical Strength: Caring for My Body

Cancer treatment takes a toll on your body. The physical side effects can be grueling—nausea, fatigue, hair loss, weight changes, and a weakened immune system. At times, my body felt like it was betraying me. But I learned that true strength isn't just about how much you can push yourself physically; it's about how you care for your body in the midst of its challenges.

I had to learn to listen to my body, to give it the rest and nourishment it needed. It was hard not to push myself too hard, but I realized that allowing my body to heal was just as important as any medical treatment. The more I honored my body, the more strength I gained. Strength isn't just about enduring—it's about nurturing and respecting yourself through the process.

4. Mental Strength: Harnessing the Power of the Mind

A huge part of my cancer journey was mental. The mind is powerful, and it can either help you survive or sabotage your recovery. There were days when fear, doubt, and negativity clouded my thoughts. But I learned that mental strength is the key to navigating those dark moments.

I started practicing positive self-talk, focusing on what I could control, and visualizing my healing. I learned to quiet the voice of fear that wanted to take over and instead fill my mind with thoughts of hope, strength, and healing. Mental strength isn't about denying your emotions or pretending everything is okay. It's about choosing to face your fears head-on, acknowledging them, and then moving past them.

5. Emotional Strength: Handling the Highs and Lows

Throughout my cancer treatment, I experienced an emotional rollercoaster. There were days of hope and optimism, and there were days of deep despair and frustration. Sometimes I felt like I couldn't bear it, but I realized that emotional strength is about allowing yourself to feel whatever comes—without letting those feelings control you.

When sadness, fear, or anger crept in, I gave myself permission to feel it. I didn't try to suppress it or pretend I wasn't struggling. But I also learned to let it pass, rather than holding onto it. Emotional strength is about accepting the ups and downs of the journey and knowing that you are allowed to feel vulnerable. You don't have to be strong every minute of every day. Sometimes, simply acknowledging your emotions is a powerful act of strength in itself.

6. Strength in Support

I also learned that strength doesn't mean doing everything on your own. One of the most surprising things about my cancer treatment was the power of support. There were times when I couldn't find the strength to keep going, but my family, friends, and medical team were there to lift me up when I needed it most.

I realized that asking for help and allowing others to support me was not a sign of weakness—it was a testament to the strength of my relationships and the power of community. Strength is knowing when to lean on others and allow them to help carry you through the difficult times. The love and support I received from my circle gave me the strength to keep fighting.

7. Spiritual Strength: Finding Faith in the Journey

Cancer treatment can make you question everything—your faith, your purpose, your very existence. There were moments when I felt completely lost, wondering if I could endure what lay ahead. But it was during these moments that I discovered the power of spiritual strength.

I leaned heavily on my faith throughout my treatment. Whether it was prayer, meditation, or simply moments of quiet reflection, I found peace in my spirituality. I didn't have all the answers, and I couldn't control the outcome, but I found strength in surrendering to something greater than myself. Spiritual strength gave me the courage to face each day with the belief that I wasn't alone—that there was a bigger purpose unfolding, even in the darkest of times.

8. Strength in Acceptance

There were parts of my journey that were beyond my control. I couldn't choose how my body would respond to treatment, how much pain I would endure, or what the future would hold. But through cancer treatment, I learned the strength of acceptance.

Acceptance isn't about giving up—it's about acknowledging the reality of your situation without resistance. It's about choosing to live in the present moment, rather than obsessing over what's to come. The more I accepted my circumstances, the more peace I found. In accepting the things I couldn't change, I gave myself permission to focus on the things I could—my healing, my mindset, and my will to keep moving forward.

9. Strength in Small Wins

During my treatment, I learned to celebrate small victories. Every day I made it through was a win. Whether it was getting through a tough round of chemotherapy, making it out of bed, or simply finding a moment of joy, I celebrated those small steps. They may have seemed insignificant at the time, but each one added up and built my strength.

Strength isn't about one big, heroic act. It's about the accumulation of small, everyday victories. Every step forward is progress, and every small win is a testament to the power within you.

10. Strength in Never Giving Up

Perhaps the most important lesson I learned about strength during my cancer journey is that true strength lies in never giving up. Even when things seemed impossible, even when the pain felt unbearable, I chose to keep going.

Giving up never crossed my mind. I knew that as long as I had breath, I had a chance. Strength isn't about never being knocked down—it's about getting back up every time you fall. It's about the decision to keep moving forward, one step at a time, no matter how difficult the path may be.

11. Strength in Gratitude

Throughout my treatment, I learned to find strength in gratitude. Even on the toughest days, I tried to focus on what I was grateful for—the moments of kindness from others, the progress I was making, and the simple joys of life. Gratitude helped me shift my perspective from what I lacked to what I had.

By practicing gratitude, I cultivated a sense of strength that kept me grounded, no matter how difficult things got. Gratitude helped me realize that there is always something to be thankful for, even in the midst of a battle.

12. Strength in Believing in My Recovery

Finally, I found strength in believing that I could recover. In the face of uncertainty, in the midst of countless treatments and setbacks, I held on to the belief that I could overcome this. That belief, that unshakable faith in my ability to heal, was one of the most powerful sources of strength during my cancer journey.

Strength isn't about knowing exactly what the future holds. It's about trusting that no matter what comes, you have the resilience and the courage to face it. Believing in your recovery is one of the strongest things you can do for yourself—and it's what will carry you through the toughest of times.

Cancer treatment tests your limits. It challenges every part of who you are—your body, your mind, your spirit. But through it all, I found a strength.

CHAPTER LVIII

The Power of Humor

Humor became one of the most unexpected and essential tools in my arsenal during my cancer journey. As I faced each new challenge—whether it was the grueling treatments, the overwhelming fatigue, or the fear that accompanied each hospital visit—I quickly realized that laughter wasn't just a way to pass the time; it was a lifeline. Humor became a way to fight back against the dark shadow that cancer had cast over my life. It gave me moments of peace, lightness, and even joy, which were crucial in maintaining the strength to keep moving forward.

Humor: A Light in the Darkness

The very first days after my diagnosis were filled with fear, confusion, and an overwhelming sense of loss. In those moments, I could barely think beyond the illness itself. But as I began to process my diagnosis, I realized that laughter had a surprising place in this journey. In the face of an unknown future, I knew that humor could help me regain some sense of control.

One of the first things Jayu did after I was diagnosed was to remind me of the importance of humor. She made it a point to keep me smiling, even when the days seemed impossible. She knew how important it was for me to find relief, even for a brief moment. There were days I would lie in bed after chemotherapy, exhausted and weakened, when Jayu would sit beside me and tell me silly stories or reenact moments from our favorite TV shows. Her ability to laugh and make me laugh—even when my body was drained—was one of the greatest gifts I could have received.

Humor helped me face the pain. It reminded me that even in the darkest hours, there was still room for light. The emotional toll of cancer can be just as devastating as the physical, and humor became my shield against the mental weight of the journey. It helped me find a small corner of relief amid the endless appointments, treatments, and hospital stays. That small corner of humor gave me the courage to face each new day with hope.

Shared Laughter: The Connection Between Cancer Fighters

During my treatment, one of the things I learned was the power of shared humor. When I was in the chemotherapy ward, I was surrounded by other patients, all of us fighting our individual battles. But in the shared experience of suffering, humor became a common language. We would exchange stories about the strange side effects of chemotherapy, the awkwardness of hospital gowns, or the funny things that happened during our long hours of treatment.

I remember one day when I was feeling particularly low—nauseous, weak, and drained—and I overheard a fellow patient joking with the nurse. She was talking about the "fashion statement" of the hospital gown and how it could use a redesign. That simple joke, one made in the middle of a difficult treatment session, made me chuckle. It wasn't a grand joke or a show-stopper, but in that moment, it made the world feel a little less heavy. It reminded me that even cancer patients—who were enduring unimaginable hardships—could find humor in the situation. And in that shared laughter, we all found a bit of strength.

Humor has the power to bond people together. During my treatment, some of the strongest connections I made weren't just about sharing stories of illness, but about sharing jokes and laughter. It made us feel human again in a situation that often stripped us of that very feeling. In a place filled with fear and pain, humor allowed us to remember that we were still individuals, not defined solely by our disease.

Humor in the Face of Fear

There were times when fear would paralyze me—fear of the unknown, fear of the treatments, and fear of the future. During these moments, I realized that humor didn't eliminate the fear, but it allowed me to confront it with a bit more courage.

One of my most vivid memories was the first time I went in for a PET scan. I was nervous, uncertain, and anxious about the results. Jayu could see the worry on my face and, in her usual way, turned it into an opportunity to make me laugh. "You're going to be fine," she said, "But hey, if you need a superhero cape for the scan, I can probably find one for you." Her words made me laugh, and for a few moments, the fear faded. It didn't make the test any less intimidating, but it gave me a bit of breathing room to take it on with a lighter heart.

It was moments like this that taught me the value of humor when fear threatened to take over. Humor gave me permission to feel human, to laugh at my fears, and to regain control when the situation felt beyond my grasp. It didn't change the circumstances, but it changed how I responded to them. It allowed me to step into the future with a little more courage and a lot more grace.

Laughing at the Absurdity of Cancer

Cancer often feels like an endless series of absurdities—things that make no sense, things that defy logic, and moments that make you question your reality. It's easy to fall into the trap of despair when you're faced with the constant barrage of treatments, appointments, and medical terms that mean nothing to you. But in those moments, laughter became a tool to cope with the madness of it all.

One of the funniest things I experienced during my treatment was the realization of how strange cancer-related appointments could be. After a few rounds of chemotherapy, I started to joke with the nurses about how I was getting to know every inch of the hospital—its waiting rooms, the smell of antiseptic, and even the funny little phrases the doctors would say. "Oh, you're back again!" the nurses would joke when I walked in. "Do you have a VIP pass now?"

The absurdity of the situation made me laugh, and in those moments, I realized just how surreal the whole experience had become. Yes, I was fighting cancer, but the world around me had become this odd little stage in which I was playing a role. Laughing at the absurdity of it all reminded me that life, no matter how hard it gets, doesn't have to be taken too seriously.

Humor as a Tool for Recovery

Even after the initial treatment phase, when I was recovering from surgeries and chemotherapy, humor continued to play an essential role. It helped me push through the challenges of post-treatment life, from fatigue to frustration. When the side effects of treatment lingered—when my body wasn't recovering as quickly as I wanted it to—humor allowed me to accept my new reality without feeling defeated.

I remember a time when I was exhausted after a long day of recovery and felt like I wasn't making progress. My body felt weak, and my energy was low. But Jayu, with her ever-present sense of humor, would turn to me and say, "Remember, the tortoise won the race. Slow and steady wins the fight." That simple, humorous reminder helped me reframe my situation. It made me laugh, and it made me realize that recovery was not about rushing but about being kind to myself, embracing the journey, and finding humor in every small victory.

Humor became an important part of my healing process. It wasn't just about laughter; it was about embracing the imperfections of life and using them to fuel my recovery. It reminded me that I didn't have to be perfect, that it was okay to laugh at myself, and that I didn't have to have all the answers. Humor made the recovery process a little less daunting, one joke at a time.

Embracing the Power of Laughter

In the end, humor didn't just help me survive cancer—it helped me embrace life again. Even after the long road of treatment, it was laughter that kept me grounded, connected, and reminded me of the beauty of living. Humor allowed me to see beyond my diagnosis and focus on the joys that still existed, no matter how small they seemed.

Laughter became a way of being. It reminded me to not take myself too seriously, to find joy even in the hardest moments, and to never underestimate the power of humor to heal. As I reflect on my cancer journey, I can confidently say that humor played a vital role in my recovery. It was the thread that wove through the darkest times and illuminated the path forward. In laughter, I found strength, resilience, and, ultimately, the courage to face each new day.

When cancer tried to take away my body, humor gave me back my spirit. And for that, I will be eternally grateful.

From Ashes To Inspiration

As I reflect on my journey, a profound sense of gratitude and awe fills my heart for all the cancer fighters and survivors who walk this path. Our stories, though unique, share a common thread—resilience. Each battle, each scar, and each tear has its place in this narrative of survival. Cancer is not merely an illness; it's a challenge to the soul, a test of character, a profound transformation. Like the phoenix rising from the ashes, we too emerge from our trials—stronger, more determined, and filled with a renewed sense of purpose and hope.

Cancer's path is not one for the faint of heart. It challenges us in ways that we never thought possible—physically, mentally, and emotionally. It tests us, shakes us to our core, and leaves us questioning our limits. The fear, the uncertainty, the relentless fatigue—all these burdens weigh heavily on the soul. But, those of us who have walked through this fire, emerged from the ashes, and carried on are bound together by a force greater than the illness itself. There is an unspoken strength that connects us all, something that cannot be measured by any doctor's scale or understood by those who have never fought this battle.

The Journey of the Cancer Fighter

To the cancer fighters still in the battle: your strength is immeasurable. Every single day you continue to fight is an act of courage. You may not feel it, but each step forward—no matter how small—is a victory. Some days, it may seem impossible to continue. The weight of the world might feel too heavy to bear. But you are not alone in this fight. Even in the most challenging moments, when it feels like the darkness is closing in, know that you are not walking this road by yourself. There is a community of warriors, just like you, standing beside you, offering their support, their prayers, and their love. Hold on to hope. Remember, even on the toughest days, your journey is a testament to the resilience that defines you. Every small victory you claim is a powerful reminder to others that it is possible to rise, no matter how hard the battle seems.

The Phoenix Within: The Strength of Survivors

To the survivors: we are the living proof that it is possible to rise from the ashes of suffering. Our scars are not marks of weakness; they are the badges of survival. They are symbols of the strength and resilience that carried us through some of the darkest times of our lives. The true power of survival lies not only in our physical recovery but in the lessons learned, the relationships built, and the emotional strength we gained from enduring adversity. Each day we live, we carry with us the power of experience, of survival, and of unwavering hope.

We are a beacon of hope for those still fighting. Every survivor is a shining example that it is possible to overcome. Every time we share our story, we light a path for someone else who feels lost in their own struggle. It's in the simple, quiet moments—those times when we stand, breathe, and walk forward—that our story speaks louder than words. Never underestimate the strength in your journey. Your experience is proof that healing is not only possible but inevitable. Hope, resilience, and life are always within reach.

To the Unsung Heroes: Families, Friends, and Caregivers

To the families, friends, and caregivers who stand beside us: your strength is our strength. You are the silent warriors in this fight, the unsung heroes who face this battle with a bravery that is often invisible to the outside world. You are the ones who lift us up when we cannot lift ourselves, who comfort us when the road ahead seems too long. Your love, care, and unwavering support are the invisible thread that binds us all together. You hold us when we break, cheer us on when we falter, and give us the strength to keep going even when we feel defeated.

Your dedication is the foundation upon which we rebuild ourselves. It's your strength, your compassion, and your sacrifice that allow us to find the courage to keep going. Without you, the journey would be far more difficult. We carry your strength with us every day as we continue to fight, and for that, we are eternally grateful.

Honoring Those We've Lost

And to those we have lost—your memory continues to live on in each of us. Your courage, your bravery, and your spirit continue to inspire us every single day. Your fight was not in vain. You have shown us what true strength is, and your legacy lives on in the hearts of those who follow in your footsteps. You lit the way for us, and now, we carry that light forward.

Cancer may take our bodies, but it cannot take our spirits. It may break us physically, but it also has the power to remake us into something stronger, wiser, and more compassionate than we could have ever imagined. You are never forgotten. Your strength is embedded in our hearts, and your fight continues to inspire the battles of those still fighting.

Rising Stronger Than Ever

There were moments when I thought I couldn't keep going. The weight of it all, the fatigue, the fear, the isolation—it all seemed too much. There were moments when I couldn't imagine a future beyond the pain and the struggle. But then, slowly, something miraculous began to happen. The darkness began to recede. The strength that I thought I had lost began to return, bit by bit. The light that once seemed so distant slowly grew brighter, until it became impossible to ignore.

I realized that cancer did not just change my body—it changed me. It made me stronger, more resilient, more determined, and more aware of the power of hope. I found strength in places I never knew existed. I found courage in the face of my deepest fears. I found joy even in the hardest of moments. I learned that no matter how dark life gets, there is always a way to rise. And when we rise together, we are an unstoppable force.

Cancer is a battle, but it is also a transformation. It forces us to confront our deepest fears, but it also invites us to redefine who we are. It may try to break us, but it can never break our spirit. From the ashes of suffering, we rise—renewed, inspired, and ready to face whatever comes next.

Your Story is Not Over

As I close this chapter, I want to leave you with this: Your story is not over. You are not defined by your diagnosis. You are defined by your strength, your resilience, and your refusal to give up. You are defined by your courage to keep fighting, to keep living, and to keep inspiring.

No matter where you are in your journey—whether you're just beginning, in the midst of treatment, or on the other side—know that you are stronger than you think. Know that you are not alone. Your story is powerful. It is your light, your hope, and your will to rise that will guide you through the toughest times. Together, we are an unstoppable force. Our collective light shines brighter than any darkness. Keep fighting. Keep living. Keep inspiring. Because together, we rise—stronger than ever.

We are more than cancer. We are survivors, warriors, and a beacon of strength to the world. Our stories are far from over, and as we rise from the ashes, we carry with us the power to inspire others, to light the way, and to show that no matter how fierce the battle, hope will always rise from the ashes.

www.ingramcontent.com/pod-product-compliance
Lightning Source LLC
Chambersburg PA
CBHW031050160726
47991CB00005B/2095